Alex Pettes
October 2010

Governing
Business & Relationships

A. Parthasarathy

First Edition 2010

ISBN No: 978-81-906179-6-3

Published by:
A. Parthasarathy
1A Landsend
Mumbai 400 006
India
www.vedantaworld.org

Printed by:
Vakil & Sons Pvt. Ltd.
Industry Manor
Mumbai 400 025
India

CONTENTS

PREFACE

All the problems that people encounter with their business and relationships converge to one rudimentary problem. It is the lack of development and use of the intellect. You remain unaware of the power and grandeur of your intellect. Make little use of it while you combat the multifarious problems of life. You are all fighting the challenging forces of the world with bows and arrows when you have an F-16 in your hangar!

The intellect and the mind are the two equipments which drive the body to act. Of the two the intellect is most powerful. It is the faculty of thinking, reasoning, judging. The mind is the seat of impulses, feelings, emotions. When the intellect guides the mind in actions then they would be discretionary, mature. And when the mind overpowers the intellect the actions would be impulsive, immature. Thus all management emanates from these two equipments. And the calibre of management would depend upon the use of the intellect in deciding the course of action.

The world today lacks the awareness of the intellect. Much less the necessity to develop it. For centuries the human intellect has been totally neglected. Causing severe damage to persons and families, corporations and countries. Yet people have not awakened to this stark reality. They remain complacent, not realising the vital role the intellect plays in human life. That all management and sound relationship must proceed from reason and judgement of the intellect rather than feeling and emotion of the mind.

The corporates mechanically follow routine practices in the conduct of their business laid down by self-styled business schools. Spouses and parents are overwhelmingly emotional than rational in their approach to each other and their children. While religious practitioners pursue dogged, pertinacious procedures set by their leaders' baseless beliefs, superstitions and rituals. The entire human race blindly adopts a life set by predecessors. The intellect, lacking development and strength, hardly plays a part in the lives of people.

Consequently, families are torn apart, business houses collapse and nations are at daggers drawn. While governing bodies in the fields of education, politics and religion helplessly gaze at the internal and external crises that humanity faces.

The human intellect can handle, harness the rigours of nature and the colossal challenges of life. But the neglect of the intellect has left human beings troubled and tortured by the slightest confrontation of the world. The celebrated English poet William Wordsworth laments on this sad state: *It grieves my heart to think what man has made of man when every flower enjoys the air it breathes.*

Furthermore, the intellect is of two kinds based on its distinct functions. They are known in Sanskrit language as *tikshna buddhi* gross-intellect and *sukshma buddhi* subtle-intellect. The gross-intellect's function is confined to the extremities of the universe. While the subtle-intellect can go beyond the universe and reach the transcendental Reality through identification with one's own Self within.

A powerful gross-intellect could with ease take care of the problems pertaining to all mundane affairs. Be it business or time management, work ethics or leadership, family relationships or stress. Whereas, the subtle-intellect identifying with the Self could gain the ultimate of all management.

Herein you are given the formula for governing the perennial confrontations of the world you live in and rising above to attain complete sovereignty over it.

A. Parthasarathy

CHAPTER I

STRUCTURE OF MANAGEMENT

Management is structured on the three basic constituents:

1. Manager — the person, subject
2. Managed — that which is dealt with, object
3. Managing — the art of relating subject with object.

Manager

The manager is one of the many roles a person plays in his life. The roles keep changing with time, place, environment, situation. You could be a manager in your office, a parent in your home, a sportsman in the field, a citizen of your country etc. At a time you may play one or more roles. For instance, you could be a manager and citizen at the same time. While you manage your business you cannot ignore your obligation as a citizen of your country. However, through the diverse roles you play in life, the person who plays these roles remains the same.

Who is the person behind the various roles? What part or parts of his personality execute the act that he takes upon himself? What determines the success of the role he is engaged in? The layperson would attribute the cause for success to one's calibre. People all over accept such generalisation and go no further. It is no doubt the calibre of the person that defines the performance in any field. But what determines the ability, competence, proficiency that go together to build the calibre of the person? That would need an examination of the individual. A study of the anatomy of a human being and the agency within him which is actually responsible in playing his roles in life.

A human is composed of Spirit and matter. Spirit is Self, the Core of the human personality. Matter comprises *vasanas*, a Sanskrit word meaning one's inherent nature, innate bent. *Vasanas* manifest as body, mind and intellect. The body perceives the sense objects through its sense organs and executes actions through its organs of action. The mind comprises impulses, feelings, emotions, likes and dislikes. And the intellect thinks, reasons, judges, decides.

The Human Constitution

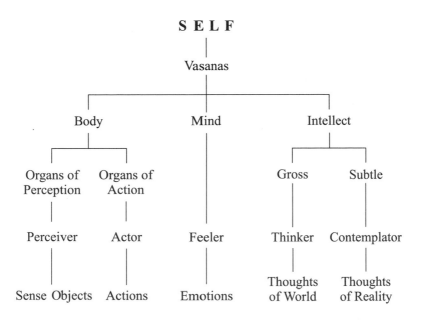

The Self merely enlivens the body to perceive and act, the mind to feel and the intellect to think. The *vasanas* determine the quality, type of perception and action, emotion and thought that emanate from the body, mind and intellect. A person with business *vasanas* will plunge into business. One with music *vasanas* will take up musical roles. Sports *vasanas* will produce a sportsman. Etcetera.

Your first obligation in life is to choose a field of activity according to your basic nature, termed in Sanskrit as *svadharma*: *sva* = one's own, *dharma* = nature. Your *svadharma* is constituted of your *vasanas*. The field of activity of your choice must fit into your *svadharma*. It is not in your interest to choose a field which is *paradharma*: *para* = alien, *dharma* = nature. The field of *svadharma* would be conducive for success, progress and growth in your life. Whereas a field of *paradharma* would be frustrating, unproductive. Imagine Roger Federer playing golf and Tiger Woods playing tennis! In fact the author of the book himself hails from a family established in shipping business. But he found a business career alien to his nature and chose to research and propagate in the field of his *svadharma*, Vedanta philosophy which he continues to date. To simplify the concept, *svadharma* would act as the tailwind and *paradharma* as headwind to an aircraft in flight. So the first lesson you learn in life is to choose a career according to your *svadharma*.

As the Self, Spirit contacts the body-mind-intellect there is manifestation of life. Just as electricity contacting an electric bulb manifests as light. The spiritual Core is homogeneous, one and the same in all human beings.

14

The variety of human beings is the result of the heterogeneity of *vasanas*. The *vasanas* manifest as the matter vestures – body, mind and intellect. And the quality and texture of these equipments differ from person to person according to the nature of one's *vasanas*.

The body is the grossest of the three. The mind is subtler than the body. And the intellect, subtler than the mind. All through the lives of human beings the Self, Spirit remains supreme, immaculate, immutable. Nothing can nor need be done to the Self. However, the skills of an individual can be improved upon by developing his material equipments. The intellect being the subtlest therefore plays the most important part in any form of management. But the educational systems today have lost track of the intellect and its vital role in human life. Consequently, the management personnel themselves have been denied the exercise of developing and strengthening their intellects.

With lack of development of the intellect, corporate gurus have been imposing their personal, sporadic views on management in well packaged literary jargons. And their books and seminars have earned bestselling statuses in a community where both the teacher and taught have been deprived of intellectual growth and strength. The blind leads the blind. The problem of humanity arises from the fact that one needs an intellect to evaluate and develop one's intellect. In truth, humans are not aware of the emaciated state of their intellect. To possess a disease in the body is quite serious. But to have a disease and not be aware of its presence could prove fatal. That is the sad state of the corporate world.

Managing

The body per se cannot act. The actions of the body emanate from one's mind and intellect. The mind and intellect constitute the managing agency which drives the body to act. Together they become the propelling force in all activities. The body no doubt executes actions. But the actions of the body are driven by either the likes and dislikes, feelings and emotions of the mind or the reason, discretion, judgement of the intellect. Examine these two possibilities arising from a single action. Offer a sweet to a diabetic person who is fond of sweets. His mind craves for it while his intellect understands he is forbidden to eat it. When his intellect is stronger than the mind, it directs the body to abstain from it. If on the contrary his mind is strong and intellect weak he would consume it and suffer the consequences thereof.

The intellect therefore must govern and guide the mind at all times. An unattended mind could become unstable and gradually lose its sanity. When the impulses, feelings of the mind drive actions without the guidance of the intellect then such actions would be *impulsive*. And when the intellect controls and directs the mind to act then those actions would be *discriminative*. Discriminative actions determine the sanity of the person. As impulsive actions displace discriminative actions he would gradually lose his sanity. The figure below shows the loss of intellectual application resulting in the deterioration of a human being.

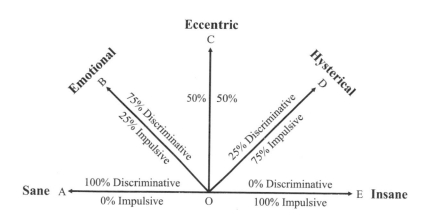

When a person's intellect supervises and guides every impulse and emotion of his mind his actions would be 100% discriminative and 0% impulsive as in position

A. He is then a perfectly *sane* person. As his intellectual supervision and guidance falls to 75%, so would his discriminative actions. And his impulsive actions rise to 25%. This ratio renders him an *emotional* person as in position B. With a further loss of intellectual application and the ratio striking 50:50 he becomes *eccentric* as in C. With only 25% of his actions covered by his intellect and 75% taken over by the mind he turns *hysterical* as in D. At the last position E when his intellect is absent, his actions totally impulsive and none discriminative, he becomes *insane*. A careful scrutiny of the world would reveal that most human beings range between emotional and eccentric. It is an appreciable loss of the intellect which no human can afford.

There is nothing wrong in possessing emotions. But to let them interfere with your intellectual judgement would be erroneous, detrimental. A weakness which has caused humans to suffer for ages. History has revealed how emotions have overpowered discretion and caused many heads to roll by. The renowned playwright, William Shakespeare has demonstrated this fatal consequence in *King Lear, Macbeth, Othello* and his other plays. Business executives are victims of this inherent weakness. They fall a prey to greed for more money, fame and power. And are lost in professional jealousy, emotional attachment to their family and a host of other self-corroding emotions. These emotions blur their discretion and judgement. While decisions falter to affect their management skills.

A businessperson's managerial calibre therefore rests on the strength of the intellect and its application to business. His intellect must not allow any form of emotional involvement or attachment to interfere with his particular role in business. That would ruin his concentration and decision making. Concentration means the intellect controlling and directing the mind in every activity. Accordingly, an executive must focus on his present action to spell success and progress in his life.

Thus all management skills reduce to self-management. And self-management depends upon the development and use of the intellect. The way to develop, strengthen the intellect is by questioning everything and not taking anything for granted. That is to think independently, originally. Hardly anyone in the world thinks, questions the fundamentals. People the world over indiscriminately follow their predecessors and suffer the consequences thereof.

CHAPTER II

ROLE OF THE INTELLECT

The world that living beings pass through is ever changing. Morning turns into noon, noon into evening and evening into night. Childhood turns into boyhood, manhood and old age. So do profit and loss, marriage and divorce, health and ill health, peace and war, life and death. Everything is in a flux of change. In and through these fluctuations and oscillations you must learn to navigate yourself towards success and peace in your life. Vedanta, the ancient Indian philosophy, helps you learn and apply this art to cruise through challenges and emerge triumphant. Just as a surfer sports with the waves lashing on the shore and comes out recreated. And the art of navigating through all facets of the challenging world emanates from self-management.

The management of affairs of the world would therefore need the application of a well-developed intellect. To the extent the intellect is developed to that level alone it can steer the mind and actions in the right direction. Whatever skills you possess will be lost if your intellect is not strong enough to hold the mind in its place. Hence you must ensure that you strengthen your intellect to maintain a perfect control over the mind for exercising your managerial skills to the optimum.

The crux of management therefore lies in strengthening your intellect. And not by merely burdening yourself with procedures laid down by management consultants bereft of the intellect. A powerful intellect alone can render your actions more objective, more productive in the roles you play in life. William Shakespeare highlights this idea in his play *Othello*. Wherein the general appointed a mathematician with no experience of warfare as captain in his army. That too, in preference to promoting his experienced lieutenant.

What is Intellect

The intellect is the ability to think freely, logically. The faculty to reason and judge without bias. When you develop a strong intellect your thinking becomes clear, your reasoning precise and judgement perfect.

Among the three living species – plant, animal and human – the human alone possesses an intellect. The plant has only a body, no mind to feel emotion nor intellect to think. Whereas the animal has a body and a mind with feeling, emotion but lacks an intellect. Only a human has all three – body, mind and intellect. A human being cannot survive without an intellect. As a human therefore your first obligation in life is to develop, strengthen your intellect.

All beings save humans have a built-in programme for them to live their lives. Their living patterns are determined by nature. Each creature lives in accordance with its fixed pattern. Wherein there is no choice of action. Only human beings are faced with the dilemma of choice. The intellect plays the all-important role to choose the right course of action at every moment of their lives. Hence to play your role in the field of management you would need a well-developed, powerful intellect.

How to Develop Intellect

Human beings have practically lost their intellect and weakly submitted to routine practices set by their predecessors. They accept past procedures in whatever they do with little thought or reason. Taking everything for granted they follow a herd instinct. And hardly question, query the authenticity of what they do and the procedures they adopt in their field of activity. Indeed they replicate the lives of animals by denying themselves the rightful choice of action.

You need to realise that your life is confronted with the dilemma of choice. The problem lies not so much in making a choice of action but on what basis do you make it. You must recognise the vital role the intellect plays in deciding the course of action in life. And that the intellect needs to be developed, strengthened to do it. But people the world over operate on feeling and emotion of the mind rather than reason and judgement of the intellect. The frail intellect yields to the impulses of the mind. It is virtually held hostage by the overpowering mind. Emotions no doubt are a part of your life. But they ought not to interfere with your intellect's judgement and decision in business and life in general.

The development of the intellect should actually commence from childhood. The child has a natural tendency to ask questions. The adults, parents must encourage children to query and clear their areas of doubt. Thus the passage through life needs to be streamlined by the process of questioning and answering. If however you have not adopted this procedure from childhood, you may start now by enquiring, questioning everything around and about you. Do not accept anything just because it has been followed for a long period of time or comes from a reputed authority. Instead, look for reason and logic in every facet of life. You then use your existing intellect to develop it further. Nobel laureate Albert Einstein has appealed to human beings: *Intellectual growth should commence at birth and cease only at death.*

The process of developing the intellect is akin to muscle building. The weak muscles of a person can be strengthened through proper exercises. With the guidance of an instructor he could in time gain a perfect body. And the very same muscles through consistent effort become firm and strong. Similarly, you should use your neglected intellect to build a powerful one.

Nature has provided every human being with an intellect. A prerogative that humans alone enjoy among all creatures. It therefore becomes their responsibility to exercise, develop, strengthen it all through life. But there has been a grave dereliction of duty on the part of humans and the intellect remains emaciated. It is the bane of the educational systems of the world. For long there has been no awareness of this serious lacuna in life. And with no effort to build the intellect people have lost the art of thinking. As a result their lives are based on groundless belief and superstition. They merely follow the assertions of irrational 'authorities' which bear no proof. Following this trend the world has reached a perilous state. Humanity must wake up from its intellectual slumber. Realise the emergent need to build the intellect. With a strong intellect alone one could combat and surmount all business, domestic and social challenges.

The author's two books *The Fall of the Human Intellect* and *The Eternities: Vedanta Treatise* have been specially designed to strengthen one's intellect. A thorough study and reflection upon their contents should help achieve this objective.

Intellect versus Intelligence

Humans round the world blunder in engaging all their time in merely acquiring *intelligence* at the expense of developing the all-important *intellect*. A serious lapse stemming from the failure to realise the distinction between *intellect* and *intelligence*.

Intelligence is built by gaining information, knowledge from external agencies, from schools and universities, from teachers and textbooks. Distinct and different from *intelligence* is the *intellect*. The *intellect* is developed through your individual effort by exercising the faculty of questioning, thinking, reasoning. Not accepting anything that does not admit logic or reason. You must realise the difference between the two. And that any amount of *intelligence* gained cannot per se build your *intellect*.

The intelligence acquired from external agencies is much like the data fed into a computer. Consider, a computer charged with a complete knowledge of fire extinguishers, firefighting and fire escapes. All the knowledge stored in its memory cannot help the computer act on its own. If the room catches fire, it cannot escape. It will perish in the flames. Likewise, all the knowledge you acquire is of no use to you without an intellect.

In truth, you need a powerful intellect to put the knowledge, intelligence gained to practical use in life. That explains why among millions of doctors graduating from medical schools only a few have discovered life-saving drugs and surgeries. Have found the remedy for terminal diseases like tuberculosis or kidney failures through transplant. So too, millions of engineers have passed out of engineering schools but a rare few designed the Panama Canal or the Eurotunnel. It is the intellect in them that renders their performance outstanding. On the contrary, all intelligence sans intellect, besides lacking success and progress ends up destroying peace and happiness in the world.

Not realising the importance of the intellect in human life people make no attempt to develop their own. Instead, they merely indulge in acquiring intelligence through surface reading of others' periodicals and publications. Few go into the depth of any literature. Education has lost its meaning and purpose. For generations human beings have turned into intelligent robots. And traversed through life without awaring, much less enquiring into the meaning and purpose of life in the world. Herbert Spencer, a profound thinker and writer, was a rare luminary. Someone had asked him if he was a voracious reader. He instantly quipped: *No sir, if I were as big a reader as others, I would have been as big an ignoramus as others.*

The world today is in a state of chaos due to the perversion in human development – all intelligence and no intellect. That explains why even highly educated businesspersons, professionals and scholars become alcoholics, rave with foul temper, succumb to worry and anxiety. It is the mind that craves for alcohol. The mind that loses its temper. Again, the mind that constantly harbours worry of the past and anxiety for the future. When the intellect remains undeveloped and weak, it is unable to control the vagaries of the mind. The frail intellect looks on helplessly as the mind devastates the person. In such a condition the business, profession and even family relationship run into shambles. On the contrary those having developed a powerful intellect, with or without academic distinction, can hold the mind under perfect control and direct action to spell success and peace in life.

The educational systems the world over must be held responsible for the debacle of the intellect. It is their primary responsibility to strike an equable balance between acquiring intelligence and developing the intellect. Only by maintaining this essential equation can governments be run, businesses conducted, professions practised and families live in peace and prosperity. The lack of intellectual sovereignty in humans has led the world to a terrible state. Nations indulge in hot and cold wars. Business houses, following sporadic views spluttered by management gurus with frail intellects, stagger and collapse. Families are torn apart with differences and divorces. Children with no direction are at sea. Confusion and chaos reigns everywhere.

Acquisition and Enjoyment

The role of the intellect is not limited to merely managing the affairs of the world. It is meant to lead you to the state of absolute peace and happiness. Bereft of intellectual guidance, humans spend their entire lifetime in acquisition and enjoyment. They crave to acquire wealth, fame and power and indulge in enjoying what they have acquired. This exercise goes on and on until their death. None knows what exactly one wants and yet the chase never ends. Few realise that it is not possible to gain true and lasting satisfaction, satiation through acquisition or enjoyment. You need a powerful intellect to help you discover what exactly you seek in life and how to achieve it. By constant application of the intellect you gain the objectivity to steer your passage through life faultlessly and reach the state of absolute fulfilment.

Human pursuits are mere attempts to find peace and happiness be it through commission or omission. A strong intellect alone will help set the right direction for you to attain that end. In the absence of a well-developed intellect people rush into the world for material gains to find inner peace and satisfaction. Every human craves to earn and accumulate more wealth, fame or power. Little does he realise that the material gains have never given nor can ever give the peace, contentment and happiness he seeks.

People realise too late that there is no limit to acquiring wealth. Billionaires, with money accumulated to near limitless levels, fall a prey to what is labelled as Wealth Fatigue Syndrome. Not knowing where they have erred they aggravate the problem in augmenting their wealth further. They scratch the wound that bleeds. The European philosopher of the first century, Seneca wisely states: *The acquisition of riches has been to many not an end to their miseries, but a change in them. The fault is not in the riches, but the disposition.*

Abundance of wealth drives the opulent to indulge in excessive spending. In the initial stages their purchases are sparked by greed and envy at others who possess more. A man with a 200 ft yacht desires a 500 ft one and gets it. Another with a four-seater plane acquires a luxury jet. The seesaw of discontent and content persecutes them all through life. Thus they go on a spree of purchasing houses and holiday homes, cars and yachts, planes and helicopters as children purchase toys. They find their entertainment for a while and soon get tired. And throw them away only to acquire new toys. All the shopping is a vain attempt to cover their boredom and depression. The madness is never attended to, much less overcome. None is aware that uncontrollable desires cause the suffocating dullness and isolation that the wealthiest suffer from. Ironically, they themselves have no clue of what they are going through. They need to look at those who have less and realise their own fortunate position. However, there is no taboo to acquisition except to exercise control, regulate the mind's indiscriminate craving for wealth.

Those who run after name and fame meet with the same fate. In the initial stage people crave to gain even a little recognition from others. They would love to have their name or picture appear in the newspaper, magazine or television. And would pay a price to achieve it. Humans are victimised by the desire to be known and praised by others. A petty satisfaction from a petty desire. It all stems from an inferiority or superiority complex. You get over this pettiness by realising the great plan of nature. The world is made up of a variety of beings. Each has a part to play in this well orchestrated world. None big or small, important or unimportant in such a perfect setup. Why have any complexes? Let each play his role as best as he can in this orchestra. That would bring about the beautiful melody of existence in the world.

The desire for power again is insatiable. The more the power a person gains the more he craves for. It takes him up in a spiral and ultimately destroys him. History has revealed how this craving has devastated several leaders and countries. Ironically, real power emerges from selflessness in a person. The more unselfish he is the more power he commands. No selfish person can wield power for long. Yet the masses go about selfishly seeking power in the world.

The next motivation that drives humans after acquisition is to enjoy their material gains by contacting them. As a result they plunge into indiscriminate indulgence and gradually lose the pleasure derived therefrom. And reach a point when any further contact gives no pleasure at all. A state known as neutralisation.

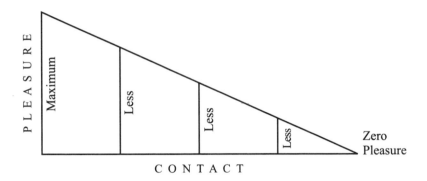

Thus through indulgence the superrich get neutralised to the enjoyment of material gains. Their life drags into a state of utter monotony. You need a powerful intellect to realise that only through proper regulation and moderation does one really enjoy the world. Your intellect must constantly check and control indiscriminate indulgence to regulate, moderate your sensual activity. You would then maintain the level of enjoyment all through life.

With all the apparent consequences of senseless pursuits, people with little intellect devote their lifetime to acquiring material wealth, fame and power and trying to find enjoyment in what they acquire. Without intellectual guidance they virtually isolate themselves and are lost in desperation. In truth, he who is not content with what he has, would not be content with whatever he acquires.

William Cowper, in his outstanding poem *The Pineapple and the Bee*, portrays such madness in human pursuits. The poem narrates how a bee tries in vain to penetrate a glass frame to reach the pineapples arranged therein. The poet compares the bee's desire for the pineapple to a human's craving for wealth and enjoyment. He gives two examples of this weakness in humans. The one, a maid's desire for jewellery behind the show-glass and the other, a man's desire for a woman passing by in a chariot. Human beings the world over squander their lifetime pursuing their insatiable desire for possession and enjoyment. The poem shows how desires lead some to frustrate themselves with vain hopes; others to break barriers and suffer the consequences thereof. While the wise with a clear intellect finds peace and happiness even in adverse environment and circumstance. The poem:

The Pineapple and the Bee

The pineapples in triple row,
Were basking hot and all in blow,
A bee of most discerning taste
Perceiv'd the fragrance as he pass'd,
On eager wing the spoiler came,
And search'd for crannies in the frame,
Urg'd his attempt on ev'ry side,
To ev'ry pane his trunk applied,
But still in vain, the frame was tight
And only pervious to the light.
Thus having wasted half the day,
He trimmed his flight another way.
　Methinks, I said, in thee I find
The sin and madness of mankind;
To joys forbidden man aspires,
Consumes his soul with vain desires;
Folly the spring of his pursuit,
And disappointment all the fruit.
While Cynthio ogles as she passes
The nymph between two chariot glasses,
She is the pineapple, and he
The silly unsuccessful bee.
The maid who views with pensive air
The show-glass fraught with glitt'ring ware,

Sees watches, bracelets, rings, and lockets,
But sighs at thought of empty pockets,
Like thine her appetite is keen,
But ah the cruel glass between!
Our dear delights are often such,
Expos'd to view but not to touch;
The sight our foolish heart inflames,
We long for pineapples in frames,
With hopeless wish one looks and lingers,
One breaks the glass and cuts his fingers,
But they whom truth and wisdom lead,
Can gather honey from a weed.

— William Cowper

The Human Temperaments

Human beings have distinct and different natures. Which fall under three broad temperaments known in Sanskrit language as *sattva*, *rajas* and *tamas*. Every human being is composed of all the three temperaments.

Tamas is the state of inertia. A person in *tamas* is lethargic, lackadaisical, indifferent, heedless. Indisposed to any form of activity. In a mood of sloth and sleep. Bereft of emotional or intellectual expression he hardly responds to the world.

Rajas is being passionate and agitated. It expresses as desire-ridden activities. A person in *rajas* is attached and involved in worldly affairs. Rushing, hurrying and worrying all the time.

Sattva is the finest human temperament of equanimity and serenity. A person in a state of *sattva* remains poised, mature, contemplative, objective. Detached from worldly involvement and excitement.

Sattva, rajas and *tamas* constituting an individual in different proportions accounts for the heterogeneity of human beings. The predominance of *sattva* in a person renders his intellect clear and sharp. Whereas, with *rajas* predominating, a person is prone to acquiring intelligence at the expense of developing the intellect. Today's world, replete with *rajas*, is all intelligence and no intellect. And where *tamas* saturates a person he has neither intelligence nor intellect.

Whatever be the *sattva* content in a person, it surfaces in the early hours of the morning between 4 am and 6 am. The *rajas* and *tamas* components in him lie low during that period. When the *sattvik* time is over, his *rajas* content rises to the surface of his personality and predominates through daytime between 6 am and 6 pm.

During that period the other two temperaments remain relatively dormant. And *tamas* emerges at night from 6 pm to 4 am. When *sattva* and *rajas* are practically inactive. This law of nature holds good for one and all in the human species.

The law is apparent in the behavioural pattern of humans throughout the world. Since *sattva* manifests in a person between 4 am and 6 am he is more composed, thoughtful and objective during those hours. Interestingly, the predominance of *sattva* in the person wakes him up early in the morning. As for *rajas*, it is seen manifest as frenzied activity during daytime between 6 am and 6 pm. And *tamas* manifests after 6 pm as indulgence in intoxicants, gambling and other senseless activity.

Hence literature composed during *sattvik* time would be far more creative and valuable than that composed during any other time of the day. But the modern trend everywhere is to sleep late and wake up late. And literature produced during *rajasik* and *tamasik* time would naturally lack lustre. Since there is poor participation of the intellect in its production. The efforts of modern writers have been mere recycling of intelligence with hardly any creativity of the intellect. And their writings wanting in substance. The world needs writers with powerful intellect to put in the best effort to think and compose their literature at *sattvik* time. The readers will then be able to understand and apply the knowledge therein in their lives. Enrique Jardiel Poncela, a Spanish novelist wisely pronounces: *When something can be read without effort, great effort has gone into its writing.*

CHAPTER III

LIFE IN FOCUS

Life is defined in Sanskrit as *anubhava dhara* meaning 'a stream of experiences'. Experiences flowing continuously is one's life just as water flowing is a river. The quality and quantity of experiences determine the nature of life. If your experiences are happy your life is happy. If dynamic, your life is dynamic. If dull, it is dull. As the experiences so the life. Therefore, to bring about a change in your life you must change your experiences. That necessitates a study of the constituents of an experience.

An experience is a unit of life. It is constituted of you and the world. You are the *subject*. The world is the *object*. When you come in contact with the world, when *subject* meets *object* there arises an experience. And experiences flowing one after another determine your life. With an idea of making human life better, more comfortable and peaceful, two sets of investigators emerged. One set worked upon the *object*, world. They were the *objective scientists*. The other set worked upon the *subject*, you. And they were the *subjective scientists*.

Objective Scientists

The *objective scientists* visualised the world under three broad facets: wealth, people and nature. And classified themselves under these three categories as economist, politician and scientist. The economist dealt with the wealth of the world. The politician with the people. The scientist with nature. Working in their respective fields they collected data, studied and reflected upon the data, drew intelligent conclusions and classified them as laws pertaining to their field of enquiry. Thus each of them went about methodically, scientifically and laid down laws in economics, politics and science. These were the *objective scientists* dealing with the *object*, world.

The *objective scientists* have no doubt worked tirelessly to make this world a better place to live in. They continue to do so without reference to what their efforts have yielded. They have failed to realise their labours have produced little peace and harmony to the people. As they have shown no interest in correlating their efforts to the end results. Ironically, their labour seems to have created more disquiet and disharmony in the world. They go about their business like an industry exercising no quality control over the products manufactured. And continue to indiscriminately work in their units even as the results accruing therefrom are poor and need correction. Though the final objective of these scientists is to produce comfort, peace and harmony in the society the results have turned out to be just the opposite.

With all the economic, political and scientific advancement the people are in a state of stress and strain and the world in confusion and conflict. Unmindful of the worldwide unrest the objective pursuits are encouraged and funded liberally without the intellectual surveillance on the impact of their achievements.

Subjective Scientists

As opposed to the above indiscriminate pursuits, from time immemorial the *subjective scientists* in India worked upon the *subject*, you. They delved deep into the human personality and discovered the Core, the supreme Self within. Thus prepared human beings not merely to face the challenges of the external world but to find true peace and happiness within oneself.

The *subjective scientists* also went about their work methodically, scientifically. They collected data on the human personality, studied and reflected upon the data, drew intelligent conclusions and formulated them as laws pertaining to the individual. These laws governing the human being constitute *Vedanta*. *Vedanta* is a Sanskrit word derived from *veda* knowledge and *anta* end. Etymologically, *Vedanta* means the end of knowledge. A knowledge which penetrates into the deep recesses of the human personality and reveals the supreme Self within. A study of the inner personality and its application in the world is essential for one to find peace and prosperity in life.

Paradox in Life

A careful scrutiny of the world would reveal that action and peace do not coexist. Where there is action, production and prosperity there is no peace and contentment. And where there is peace and contentment there is hardly any action, production, prosperity. The western world bristles with external activity and is affluent but lacks inner peace. While the eastern world rests in relative peace but lacks action and affluence. It is a strange paradox affecting human life. Which runs through the country, community and individual. At the individual level the more active, wealthy a person is the more stressed he is. Vice versa. The inactive, less wealthy is relatively free from stress and strain in life. Is this a law of nature or brought about by humans upon themselves? Vedanta provides a clear answer to this question. Every human being creates his own world. You are the architect of your fortune or misfortune. You make yourself, you mar yourself.

Humans alone are blessed with the choice of action. All other species of creation are provided with a specific mode of life for them to live by and die. Their eating habits, their mating habits, in fact their entire behavioural pattern is clearly defined. They have no choice of action. In a way they are protected by nature. Whereas, humans are faced with the dilemma of choice all through their life. And they are endowed with an intellect to exercise the choice of action. But in the world today the human intellect has been totally neglected and is in a deplorable state. It has remained undeveloped, emaciated for long. And the entire human race has been acting from likes and dislikes of the mind rather than by reason and judgement of the

45

intellect. That has caused immeasurable damage to humanity and the world.

As a result of their impulsive behaviour human beings are attached to their worldly possessions and relationships. En masse they are mentally bound to objects and beings, to their business, family, religion, to virtually everything they contact. These attachments have proven deadly. Those that are bound to the world suffer the pangs of attachment. The solution to this perennial problem is to develop your intellect and use it. You need a strong intellect to govern the impulses and emotions of the mind and avoid any form of preferential attachment.

Initially when a person's mind is attracted towards an object or being his thoughts start flowing in that direction. The stream of thoughts connecting the person to that object or being creates the attachment for it. Where there is no such indiscriminate thought flow there can be no attachment. He remains detached, poised, objective in life. And through objectivity alone can one command peace, success and prosperity.

Attachment arises from one's selfishness. When you relate to the world with a self-centred motive your thoughts run towards objects and beings. You develop initially an attachment for them. And as the thoughts grow stronger, the thicker stream of thoughts creates a desire for their possession and enjoyment. Thus you develop manifold desires. The bulk of them remain unfulfilled causing mental agitation. You suffer the stress of frustrated desires. Lose peace and poise in your life.

Your attachment and desire are unending. They could be related to the external world or your physical body, mind, intellect or the religion you follow. Depending upon the direction of your desires you adopt different personalities. Thus, when uncontrolled desires run after the world you become a materialistic person. And when they are related to your physical body, you turn into a sensualist. Unattended desires at the mental level render you impulsive, emotional, possessive. At the intellectual level your desires for acquiring information, knowledge makes you intelligent. And at the religious level, when your desires are confined to your personal religion alone you turn into a fundamentalist, fanatic, extremist.

Opposed to all such worldly pursuits the rare one directs his thoughts to the supreme Reality. He seeks the Reality in the Self within to attain Self-realisation. The Abode of absolute fulfilment, peace and happiness. It would be in your interest to find out where your focus lies and study the consequences thereof. More so, to change your focus to a better and more meaningful life. Ultimately gain true Enlightenment.

Who is a Materialist

A person is adjudged a materialist or not by the value he confers upon material wealth. He who carries much value for material wealth and regards it as a primary aspect of life would be considered a materialist. Whereas one who realises material wealth as trivial and trifling regardless of the quantum he possesses and understands its limitation in one's life is no materialist.

Who is a Sensualist

A sensualist also is not judged by the extent of his physical contact with sense objects or his enjoyment thereof but by the way his mind relates to them. When the mind is irresistibly drawn towards the sense objects of the world and to the pleasures thereof, he would be a sensualist even if he physically abstains from them. Whereas another who places sense objects and the pleasures accruing from them in their true perspective, realises their ephemeral nature and maintains a suzerainty over them, he is no sensualist even if he were to be amidst sense objects and enjoying them.

Who is Emotional

Those whose desires are focused at the mental level become involved in the affairs of the world. They develop attachment, possessiveness towards whatever they contact. As a result they run into moods of passion and suffer from stress. Living a life of mental tension they invariably succumb to depression. The mind being tensed with agitation the intellect loses its focus upon any form of activity. This class of people who live at the mental level without intellectual supervision becomes emotional, impulsive, eccentric. Thus lacking intellectual application and concentration they ruin their business, their family relationship and social obligation.

However, mere possession of emotions does not render a person emotional. He may have deep emotions and keep them well under the control of his intellect. If this be so, with the intellect governing the expression of emotions, he would not be classified as an emotional person.

Who is Intelligent, who Intellectual

Those whose desires run at the intellectual level find their entertainment therein. They merely acquire information, knowledge of the external world and gain pleasure, satisfaction in it. Their pursuit ends there. Goes no further. As a result they gather intelligence. Such people become storehouses of information and knowledge of different facets of the world. And use that for making a living in the multifarious fields of activity.

Rare indeed are those that are truly intellectual. Who rise above their desires, their curiosity just to know things and maintain a sense of objectivity in life. They do not fall a prey to intellectual entertainment. Instead go into the depth of the literature they read. Interestingly, the majority of humans do not have the habit of reading. And those in the minority who read, read linear. Just go through the length of the literature. Browse through volumes without caring to reach the depth of any. They are content to indulge in intellectual surveillance for their pleasure. They are the intelligent ones but far from being intellectual.

An intellectual is one who uses his intellect to think, to reflect freely, independently without being biased by his predecessors' views and opinions. He thus makes good use of his intellect to develop and strengthen it. And with a powerful intellect he could run any business he takes up, keep himself and his family happy and create harmony in his society.

Above all, he could use the intellect to explore his inner layers and get to the Core of his personality.

Who is Religious, Spiritual

Those whose desires operate at the religious level become attached to their particular religion. They deprive themselves of an analytical and rational approach to religion. And merely follow blind beliefs, baseless superstitions and indiscriminate rituals. The desires even at this level are focused to gain their personal, self-centred interests. The general trend among religious practitioners is to go to their respective shrines to pray either for more wealth or find solace for the disturbed mind or satisfy a curiosity. Their prayers have become mere pursuits of mundane benefits. They hardly rise above these selfish demands to pursue the transcendental Reality in the Self within. Such people are far removed from being religious, spiritual.

The truly religious, spiritual are those who rise above personal desires and pursue the supreme Self within. They steadfastly use religion, religious texts and practices to seek the Self. Maintain their objectivity and religious tolerance without falling prey to fanatic attachment to a particular religion.

Human beings are thus virtually enmeshed in the web of desires operating at the different levels of their personality. Rare indeed is one who frees oneself from these desires, functions detachedly in the passage through life, to seek spiritual Enlightenment. Deprived of an ideal in life they lack the objectivity to treat the world in a spirit of dispassion. You must therefore set an ideal and learn to function dispassionately to reach the higher echelons of spirituality.

William Shakespeare drives home this point in his great message: *All the world's a stage, and all the men and women merely players; they have their exits and their entrances.*

Regardless of what you do or how you are engaged in your life remember there is no peace and happiness in the external world. True happiness lies within you. You can find it in your Self. Even as you fulfil your obligations at work and home.

CHAPTER IV

TECHNIQUE OF TIME MANAGEMENT

Time management is a misguided nomenclature. There is no such thing as time management. You cannot deal with time as such. Stretch the day to more than 24 hours or the year to over 365 days. However, a nagging problem that business executives face today is a self-imposed paucity of time. They grumble perennially at the lack of time. And their work input is impaired by hurrying and worrying all through life.

The pressure of time constraint builds up in industrialists, business executives, professionals, everybody. Time management has become a real menace to one and all regardless of the volume of work involved. The turnover of their businesses could range from a few hundred thousand to billions. But they all have loads of work hanging over them. They work late hours. Or carry work home in their briefcases or heads. And suffer from hypertension and sleepless nights. A business virus that is destroying human life. Yet few have gone into the core of the problem. Much less resolved it.

A careful scrutiny of the problem would reveal that it stems not from management of time but from the management of work undertaken. Thus when one complains of time management one actually means work management. To complete a quantum of work in a given time. And that needs the discipline of proper planning and programming. Hence the universal cry of time management is actually a reference to work involved. People are rushing to meet the deadline for completion of their assignment. They make desperate attempts to achieve it and invariably fail. The reason for their failure is the improper balancing of the equation between workload and time. In customising work with available time. Which needs the organisational skill to plan their actions well in advance. By practising this discipline they would have time at their command.

However those at work cannot conceive that the problem of completing their business in time is internal. They believe it lies in a host of external factors. In the workload, in their working conditions, the cooperation of their colleagues etc. None realises that the problem lies within oneself. That one needs to manage oneself before attempting to manage anything external in life. One can accomplish this when the intellect maintains a perfect control over the mind and its digressions. That is self-management. The whole exercise of time management therefore boils down to self-management. The corporate personnel must recognise it as a prerequisite for conducting their business. Not realising this they have denied themselves the development of the intellect. And lack self-management.

In effect, the concept of time management reduces to work management and work management to self-management. In mathematical language:

Time management = Work management = Self-management

What is Self-management

Self-management lies in streamlining one's inner personality. The human personality is constituted of an outer body and two inner equipments known as the mind and intellect. The mind is made up of feelings and emotions, likes and dislikes. The intellect is the faculty to think, reason, judge, decide. The intellect maintaining its governance over the mind's activity is self-management. The mind can desire, demand anything in life. It has no direction or dimension. It constantly digresses from its present occupation. The intellect's role is to control the vagaries of the mind and direct it to the point of its application. When your intellect thus asserts its suzerainty over the mind you have secured self-management. Without self-management, the uncontrolled mind can ruin your business, home and environment. Yet people the world over in their ignorance pamper, nourish the mind's exploits. And allow it to grow into massive proportions while totally neglecting the intellect. They become innocent victims of the dire consequences of their own actions.

Action is the insignia of life. The body executes action but it cannot act on its own. Actions of the body are propelled either by the mind or intellect. Those that are driven by the mind alone without the governance of the intellect are impulsive and those directed by the intellect, discretional. A person acting impulsively is like a drunken driver at the wheel of a car. And acting with discretion would be sober driving. Like drunken driving, impulsive actions could prove detrimental, even fatal.

The mind is fickle, unsteady, restless. It tends to worry over the past or become anxious of the future. The nature of the mind being inconstant it needs a powerful intellect to focus its attention on the present occupation. Hence, it is of prime importance to develop, strengthen the intellect to be able to manage the wavering mind and fit your work into the available timeframe. Self-management therefore becomes essential for venturing into any form of management.

Plan, Programme your Life

The technique of time management involves initial planning and programming of your life's activity. Designing your plan of action for a lifetime. At the very beginning you ought to decide what you want to achieve in life. What is the purpose, goal, ideal you have set to work for. Thinking on those lines you must fix your life's goal/s. It could be to become a millionaire or win an Olympic medal, to find the cure for cancer or eradicate poverty in the world etc. Having set a clear project the next step is to structure your course of action. Plan and programme your work methodically to achieve your objective. Those who cannot conceive the entire span of life and do not programme their actions live from moment to moment, day to day. Such people would fall a prey to the constant pressure of work and time.

Assess Work Related Factors

For the execution of your life's plan of action you must primarily assess the factors that are related to work undertaken. Those that are connected with and could influence your planned course of action. The following are some of the common factors that are work related:

1. *Svadharma* one's own nature and *paradharma* alien nature of yourself and of those you work with.

2. Choice of project with reference to your capacity and the time available to achieve it.

3. Required material and human resources at your disposal.

4. Spirit of cooperation prevalent in the project.

5. Force majeure that could interfere with the course of action.

Etcetera.

Svadharma and Paradharma

Svadharma is your basic nature and *paradharma*, a nature different from yours. Before you decide on your life's project you must ensure that it is aligned to your fundamental nature *svadharma* and not to something alien *paradharma*.

Your primary obligation in the selection of your project would therefore be to find a field you are naturally inclined to. Which would be most conducive to your mental and intellectual constitution. Into which you would slide in and enjoy working. Wherein you would be inwardly satisfied, comfortable even if the external factors are challenging, opposing. Thus, a person with an engineering tendency does not choose a medical field. Vice versa. A person with a business tendency does not take to philosophy. Vice versa. This preparation is necessary not for you alone but the colleagues you work with. Hence you must put in your effort wherever possible to select personnel having the right temperament for the work undertaken.

Your Capacity and Time Available

The project you choose in life must be realistic.

By ensuring that it is within your capacity to accomplish and you have the adequate time to complete it. Those who heedlessly take on targets beyond their capacity or with inadequate time would be unrealistic in their approach to work. Having erred initially they try to make up by working harder, spending longer hours and end up with the perennial complaint of time management. But the one with a strong intellect defines his work with the parameters of his individual capacity and adequate timeframe. That would be a great help in solving the problem of time management.

Material and Human Resources

You may choose the right type of activity according to your *svadharma*. Assess your capacity and time properly. And set a realistic target. With all that preparation you could run into difficulty if you fail to assess the material and human resources available. The resources may lack in quality or quantum. That would again impede your work. Cause problems in completing your assignments. Hence you should ensure you have the right quality and quantity of the resources required as you embark on a project.

Spirit of Cooperation

In assessing the requirement of human resource numbers are not the only criterion. One needs to look into the mental attitude of the colleagues at work. It is important that everyone works in a spirit of cooperative endeavour. Maintaining the right mental climate in the entire workforce of the project. That arises when all of them work for the growth and progress of their corporation rather than their focus on salary and perks. On the contrary, if the members of a unit are self-centred, selfish in their approach to work it would lack the cooperative spirit and ruin the growth of the unit.

It is important to examine whether one has a personal or impersonal interest at work. A personal, selfish motive spoils the quality of work and the unit one is engaged in. The right attitude is an impersonal interest directed to the overall wellbeing of the organisation. Such dedication for a larger cause has to be initiated by the leader of the unit. If a leader with no self-centred motive works for the success and progress of the organisation his colleagues will naturally follow the trait. It would be futile for a leader to solicit the cooperation of the workers when he does not take the lead. It is an impeccable truth of life: *Whatever the leader does that alone others would do; whatever standard he sets that they would reach.*

Thus the spirit of cooperative endeavour maintained in an organisation is most conducive for achieving its objective.

Force Majeure

The precautionary measures enumerated above are within one's capacity to enforce. Adopting these measures one should be able to comfortably complete the set project. However with all the planning and programming, one may encounter yet another unforeseen impediment. It could be a natural calamity, a force majeure upsetting a well projected plan of action. A fire, flood, pestilence or other. Therefore to ensure time management it would be wise to make a reasonable estimate and allowance for such emergency. And thereby provide adequate time for completing the project.

One should also be prepared to accommodate other unexpected events like personal illness, family and social obligations impinging upon the time assigned for the project. Intelligent planning and programming of business should necessarily provide for these contingencies as well.

Plan Life's Project Backward

The general trend among planners is to project their work schedules forward in life. People work out their plan of action day to day, week to week etc. 'What have I to do today', 'What have I to do this week, this month.' Thus people the world over adopt a forward planning. Which lacks the foresight into the distant future. With no clear objective in life or proper planning they run into impediments and obstacles causing embarrassment, disappointment at work.

An essential aspect of time management is to initially conceive and decide what you wish to achieve in your lifetime. Which may be one or more projects. You could aspire to be a successful businessperson and a national player in a particular sport. Whatever they be, you must decide on your life's project/s and evaluate the time available for you to accomplish it. Having decided on your life's project you must plan to execute it backwards. To cite an example, you may have a clear mission and an estimate of say, thirty years to complete it. To achieve that you must first divide the work into several parts and fit them discreetly into multiple timeframes. In effect, as your project requires thirty years for its completion, you must initially set the quantum of work that needs to be covered in the first fifteen years and what in the second fifteen. And to complete the first quantum in fifteen years you must further project what is to be accomplished in the first five years. Following the same procedure fix your plan of action for three years, two, this year. Having decided on what is to be done in the first year, programme your work for the next six months, one month, this week, today. Likewise, plan your line of action for the second quantum at the end of the first fifteen years. Thus by adopting the way of programming backwards you would project a perfect line of action. Having devised the line of action start executing its details step by step. You should then have all the time at your command.

Programme Line of Action

You could have one or more projects resolved for life. Prepare the breakdown of the projects in diminishing timeframes. Having set this up, fix the priorities for the works that go with them. And follow the order of priority. Haphazardly performing the works in a programme of action will impair the conduct of sound business.

Another important facet of business management is to be steadfast, consistent in what you do. Consistency of purpose gives the finishing touch to a well programmed business schedule. Your actions then gain power and strength. You observe this phenomenon in nature. Like water flowing or wind blowing in one direction gathers power to generate electricity.

24 Hours for All

Whatever one does, wherever that be, one has only 24 hours in a day. While the quantum remains the same for one and all the quality of time changes through the day. Few are aware of the distinct and different quality of time appearing in the course of a day. Consequently, you could end up doing the right things at the wrong time and wrong things at the right time. That would significantly affect the work output.

Every human being round the world is constituted of three different mental temperaments known as *sattva, rajas* and *tamas.* Each has a distinct character of its own. *Sattva* is of the highest quality. *Rajas* is lower. And *tamas,* the lowest.

Sattva is the state of mind in equanimity, serenity. Free from worldly entanglement and consequent mental agitation. When one is poised, mature, objective in life.

Rajas is the state of mind replete with desires, passionate and agitated. Which expresses as frenzied actions. And entangles one in the affairs of the world.

Tamas is the state of inertia. Expressing as lethargy, indolence, indifference. With no intellectual conviction to pursue. No emotional feeling to manifest. And hardly responding to the world.

Sattva, rajas and *tamas* combined in different proportions constitute an individual. The varied combinations account for the entire range of human beings. The law of nature is that the *sattva* temperament in a person surfaces in the early hours of the morning between 4 am and 6 am. And *rajas* manifests during the course of the day from 6 am to 6 pm. While *tamas* emerges after 6 pm.

As a result of this law whatever be the *sattva* content one is relatively calm and composed, reflective in the early hours of the morning. Whereas, during the day *rajas* drives everyone to desire-ridden activities. And at the end of the day *tamas* makes one indulge in intoxicants, gambling and other irresponsible, heedless behaviour.

Businesspersons and professionals must realise that their work requires reflection, planning and programming. And that is best achieved in the early hours of the morning. It is of vital importance for those who teach and practise the principles of management to observe this law of nature. But the sad plight of the present era is that none is aware of this fundamental requirement. Consequently, their thinking and writing have all emerged well beyond the *sattva* time. And their management lacks depth and direction.

CHAPTER V

VALUE SYSTEMS FOR POSITIVE LIVING

The world today is bereft of the fundamental values of life. Humanity has lost its morality and culture. And along with it peace and harmony. There is widespread internal and external disturbance everywhere. People all over are heading for self-destruction. Humans alone can avert this tragedy by resurrecting the lost values.

The values of life have to be clearly defined, learnt and imbibed by one and all. They help you to keep peace and harmony within and in the society at large. And prepare you to handle any form of external management. You could then render your actions more productive and your mind more peaceful.

At present the world is tossed between action and peace. Where there is action people have lost their peace of mind. And where there is peace there is hardly any action. A paradox that is manifest in human life at all levels the world over. Among nations, communities and individuals. Even in an individual you hardly find a dynamic businessperson or professional enjoying inner composure and peace. Nor a contented, peaceful person engaged in dynamic activity. Thus seldom do action and peace go together. Yet, the beauty and grandeur of the human race is to be energetic and enterprising externally while maintaining perfect peace and harmony internally. It therefore becomes essential for humanity to imbibe the right values in life.

Fundamental Values of Life

Some of the more important values for you to study carefully and apply them while managing the different facets of life's activity are: Action, Direction, Objectivity, Duties, Not Rights, Giving, Not Taking and Gratitude.

Action

Action is the insignia of life. None can remain without acting. Everyone is drawn to activity according to one's natural temperament. If however you choose to avoid action and remain idle your life would deteriorate, lead to self-destruction. Nevertheless, the general tendency in human beings is to laze, shirk work. They look forward to weekends and vacations. Not realising that living a lethargic life ultimately turns out to be monotonous and tiring.

Those who seek work do so only to make a living. Their motive is self-centred, selfish. When you work thus with selfish desires you entertain worries of the past and anxieties for the future. Which saps your energy. Worry and anxiety causes fatigue. You soon become exhausted at work. And you believe that work is tiring. This is far from the truth. Work can never tire you. What actually tires you is your worry over the past and anxiety of the future. That explains why children being free of worry or anxiety never get tired.

Human actions can be classified under three broad categories: Selfish, Unselfish and Selfless.

1. *Selfish Action* is action propelled by one's egocentric desire. To satisfy a self-centred interest, to gain individual benefit. Such activities are directed to mere personal acquisition and enjoyment.

2. *Unselfish Action* is action driven by an unselfish desire to serve a common cause. It could be to benefit one's corporation, community or country. The motive then loses its selfish stigma. Instead one embraces the general welfare of people.

3. *Selfless Action* is action performed in a spirit of renunciation. When one identifies with the supreme Self. When there is no egocentric desire propelling action. No anxiety to gain benefit. It is work for work's sake. Such actions are dynamic and spread peace in the society. The renowned Swami Rama Tirtha decries the self-centredness of humans: 'Why attach personal motives to work.' 'Just do what you ought to do.' Everything in this cosmos functions detachedly in a spirit of service and sacrifice. The sun gives light and vitality. So does the earth yield vegetation. A human being alone entertains motives for action. His desire-ridden actions lack lustre and cause turmoil in him and the world around.

Therefore, every human should change his lifestyle from selfish to unselfish and gradually rise to the level of selfless activity. Your actions then reach the pinnacle of perfection. Attaining that state you act tirelessly in the world while maintaining mental composure and peace. A state which fits into the famous words of Swami Rama Tirtha: *Intense work is rest.*

Direction

Gearing oneself to action is no doubt the first requirement in life. But action could lose its value if not given a proper direction. Hence you must examine the nature of your work. Analyse the reason and purpose of the activity you are engaged in. What are you working for? Your goal? So the next value you need to pursue is to fix an ideal for action above your self-centred interest, selfish desire. An ideal which caters to a nobler purpose, which serves a common cause directed to the welfare of fellow beings. The higher and nobler the ideal the greater the achievement in life. Having fixed the ideal let your actions pursue that. You would then have a right direction for your life's activity. Work undertaken in a spirit of dedication to a higher ideal is most satisfying, refreshing, rewarding. Such work does not require a break. You do not then look forward to weekend and vacation. Above all this, the goal of Self-realisation would be the highest ideal that a human being can aspire for and reach.

Objectivity

Positive living calls for not only action and direction but maintaining a sense of objectivity in work. You gain objectivity when the intellect maintains the pursuit of the ideal all through your actions. Your intellect does not allow the impulses and feelings of the mind to distract the actions away from the set direction. Thus must you conduct your life's activities with an impersonal attitude. The motto should be to strive, to struggle and not just crave for results. Your actions would then command success and productivity.

Learn to adopt action to obligation. Your business should confine to action alone. Do not yearn for reward, merit or fruit of action. Work well accomplished is a joy in itself. Your life then stays enriched by accomplishment of right action rather than mere outward success. Remember, pleasure or happiness lies in the garb of work. Go about your obligatory duty and responsibility in a spirit of detachment. Follow the pattern of nature. As the sun gives light, clouds bring rain, earth yields vegetation.

People do not realise the beauty and grandeur of selfless work. They act with selfish desires for worldly possession and enjoyment. Their interest lies not in work as such but in the fruit thereof. Self-centredness is the cause of human suffering and sorrow. You must learn to cast off selfish desire, personal motive to action. Remember, there is a divinity that shapes our ends. Surrender to the benevolence of nature. Render your work sacred. Let not your personal passions interfere with the general plan of Providence. Your motto in life should be 'Thy will be done', not 'My will be done.' Use your intellect thus to be detached, impersonal in your work. Your work then becomes most rewarding, entertaining, blissful. When you work objectively in a spirit of detachment the world greets you with prosperity and peace.

Duties, Not Rights

Every human being's fundamental obligation is to find his true identity in his lifetime. To discover the real Self within. That is the supreme ideal. Which transcends all material and worldly aspiration and acquisition. He who conceives and pursues that transcendental goal in life becomes free from the pressures of material achievement and sensual indulgence. In effect, he would act selflessly, objectively in any field of activity he is engaged. And his actions spell success, progress and peace in the world.

Having identified with the highest goal in life your worldly aspiration and acquisition fade into insignificance. They seem like candlelights before gorgeous sunlight. As a result the intellect becomes crystal clear as to your mundane duties and responsibilities. You can then with ease conceptualise your obligations towards yourself, your family, society and fellow beings. And fulfil them optimally with a sense of objectivity.

With your mission to discover the supreme Self you find all that the world offers to be trivial, inconsequential. Your mundane relationships cease to pressurise you anymore. You then confine your activity to two main obligations in life. *Nitya karma* daily, routine duties and *naimittika karma* occasional, special duties. You carry out these obligations detachedly with no axe to grind. You revel in just doing what you ought to do in life. With no egocentric desire driving it and no concern for the fruit accruing therefrom. Functioning thus with a perfect sense of objectivity you enjoy peace and happiness, you evolve spiritually. Besides, you command success and progress as well in the material world.

The law of nature is such that those governed by the spirit of obligatory *duties* shall flourish while those governed by *rights* shall perish. This law applies to individuals as well as collective bodies. However the present-day world is plagued with claims and demands. The concept of performing one's obligatory duties is practically dead. And the ghosts of rights are haunting the human race. As a result individuals claiming each one's right over the other end up in bitterness and separation. While societies and nations insisting on their rights are riddled with confrontation and conflict.

Everywhere the human trend is to insist on one's rights over others with least awareness of one's duties towards them. At the corporate level, management and labour are both keen on claiming each one's demands from the other. And nations unilaterally establish their rights over other nations. The plague of right and demand has destroyed the concept of duty and responsibility. And humans have fallen into total confusion and chaos.

Giving, Not Taking

Two distinct attitudes that support human actions are of giving and taking. The attitude of taking arises out of one's self-centred desires and demands. Those that are selfish have the tendency to aggrandise and accumulate wealth. And they develop possessiveness to the extent that they would not part even with what they do not need. This attitude causes stress, sorrow and suffering. Whereas, the attitude of giving is a noble value which spells the dignity and prestige of a human being. A human who has not learnt to give is no human. He reduces himself to the status of an animal. No animal can ever attempt to live up to this trait. A human alone can conceive the welfare of others at the expense of his own. The art of giving has proven to be one of the greatest human values.

In Charles Dickens' classic novel *A Tale of Two Cities*, Sydney Carton gave his life to save Charles Darnay who was wrongly implicated for treason. In another famous novel *Les Miserables* Victor Hugo highlights this noble trait: *Life is to give, not to take.* To cater to the welfare of one and all. You serve the world, the world serves you. It is an impeccable law of life. Unaware of this law people the world over make the blunder of taking, grabbing from the society. And suffer both materially and mentally.

The spirit of giving, sharing, serving endows you with peace and happiness. While that of taking, acquiring, aggrandising causes pain and suffering. You notice this phenomenon in the behaviour of children. Observe a child that gives, parts with her prized possession; there is a joy, cheer beaming in her face. While a child, possessive with her toys and trinkets, refusing to part with any, frowns and scowls at everything. You must learn to give, practise the art of service and sacrifice. Your life then is made. The attitude of giving provides you with inner peace as well as material prosperity. The more you give, the more you gain in life. And with the attitude of taking you lose both. The more you take, the more you lose. It is a law of life.

This law is apparent in the phenomenon of colours. Physics explains that an object possesses the colour it gives away. Light is composed of the seven vibgyoric colours. An object appears red when it gives away red and absorbs the other six colours. What it gives away, it gains. What it takes in, it loses. Hence, the great sage Swami Rama Tirtha pronounces: *The way to gain anything is to lose it.* If you crave for anything, develop a clinging attachment to it you lose it. And when you pursue it dispassionately, do not long for it, you gain it. In life, you cling to anything, it eludes you. Leave it alone, it follows you. That is the irony of life. You learn the art of giving, sharing, you are assured of peace and prosperity.

Gratitude

Gratitude stands out foremost among human values. In the sad state of the world today few can claim to possess this noble quality. And the human race suffers from the effects of ingratitude. The literary genius William Shakespeare denounces ingratitude as one of the worst traits in a human being. Ingratitude, he says, is stronger than traitors' arms.

Right from birth you enjoy countless blessings of nature. You are provided with oxygen to breathe, mother's milk, right temperature and pressure within and without, immaculate functioning of the sense organs, respiratory and alimentary canals etc. Thus the world greets one and all with a host of blessings all through life. But few seem aware of the benefaction lavished upon beings. Their only reaction to the endless provisions of nature is the greed to ask for more and more. Humans lack the sense of gratitude.

At the very beginning of life you must recognise all that you have been provided with. Realise your indebtedness to the world. Every human should learn to be grateful for what he enjoys. And repay through service and sacrifice to his colleagues, his organisation, society.

Remember the blessed words of Prophet Mohammed all through your life's activity: *The best of you is he who is best at repaying*. Hence, management must develop a feeling of gratitude for labour. And labour for management. One cannot survive without the help of the other. So must husband and wife, doctor and patient, lawyer and client and the host of other relationships develop a sense of gratitude for one another. The spirit of gratitude manifests as duty and responsibility rather than claim and demand. Just as the sap flowing in a tree sustains it so too must this spirit permeate in humans to sustain the species.

The Ultimate Objectives

One's success and progress in life rests on one's achievements. These achievements need to be specified and goals set to reach them. The ultimate objectives that a human should aspire for are herein spelt out to set the right direction in life. The foremost objective that defines human character is self-sufficiency. As you become more self-sufficient your happiness increases in quality and quantum. So an objective parallel to self-sufficiency is happiness. True happiness goes alongside the knowledge of Self. And Self-knowledge encompasses universal love. With the acquisition of Self-knowledge and universal love you would command absolute power and strength. Thus the ultimate objectives running parallel to one another are: Self-sufficiency, Happiness, Knowledge, Love and Power.

Self-sufficiency

Among the three species – plant, animal and human – a human being alone can aspire for and reach the ultimate objective, self-sufficiency in life. A plant is totally dependent upon the external world. It will die if there is no water at its roots. There may be enough water a few metres away but it cannot help itself even if it were to perish. A plant can never be independent, self-sufficient to take care of itself. Whereas in the animal species, birds, beasts and fishes demonstrate a certain level of independence. They migrate hundreds and thousands of miles for their survival. So are they not totally victimised by the world. They struggle and to an extent overcome the rigours of nature.

Soaring above these two species a human is the chef d'oeuvre of creation. Designed to enjoy complete freedom from the vicissitudes of nature and the fluctuations of the external world. Overcome the stern laws governing the world. He can harness nature by artificial means. Conquer space by jet speed. Supplement natural source of food with farming and agriculture. Combat disease with medicine. Control temperature and pressure. Etcetera.

Despite the exemplary prowess of the race, a human being allows himself to be persecuted by the world. Because of his identification and attachment to the body, mind and intellect. The body, mind and intellect and their perception, emotion and thought are affected by the changes occurring in the world. While the Self within remains immaculate, unaffected by those changes. But by virtue of your attachment to the material layers you are affected and suffer the sorrows thereof. Hence you need to turn introvert and identify with the Self within all through your mundane activities. You would then become less dependent upon the world and its variations. And when your identification with Self is complete you reach the state of absolute self-sufficiency. You become liberated from the trauma of the pairs of opposites such as profit and loss, joy and sorrow, honour and dishonour. You revel in ultimate peace and bliss.

Happiness

The happiness that humans seek externally is a mere progression of trial and error. None realises that the objects and beings of the world have little joy content. Yet people all over keep chasing the world to find their bits and pieces of passing pleasure. And claim to be happy. A cripple in a wheelchair believes that his happiness lies in a pair of legs. The one with legs believes happiness is in owning a vehicle. Thus the shadow of happiness moves on to wooing and possessing wealth, power, spouse, children and the rest. All along the pursuit one is left with unfulfilled desires causing mental agitation and sorrow. Few realise that true happiness lies within oneself. And humans continue to pursue happiness in the external world.

Imagine a dark spot in a picture projected on a screen. Try to remove that spot. You may wipe, scrub, wash it. It will not go. Because the spot is on the lens. Just wipe the lens, the spot instantly vanishes in the picture. Apply this simple principle in life. Let your intellect control your mind. Rise above your desires. A mind rid of desires finds peace and happiness. In the words of the English poet John

Milton, the mind can make a heaven out of hell and a hell out of heaven.

The phenomenon of finding pleasure where it does not exist is portrayed in the light seen in a reflection. The sun above is one but its reflections below are countless. Where there are reflecting media there would be reflected suns. But there is no light inherent in the reflected sun. What you see in the medium is the reflection of the light in the sun. Similarly, the objects and beings of the world do not have pleasure or joy inherent in them. What you claim to enjoy in them is a reflection of the bliss of the inner Self. Hardly anyone is aware of this stark reality. Lost in ignorance, people are groping to find their peace and happiness in the world at large.

It is time humans rise above their hallucination and find the seat of true happiness lying within oneself. The ideal way of living therefore would be to explore the inner layers of your personality to enjoy the real source of happiness within even as you go about your business in the world. It is no doubt challenging, exacting but there is no other way. The German philosopher Arthur Schopenhauer has wisely declared: *It is difficult to find happiness within oneself, but it is impossible to find it anywhere else.*

Knowledge

Acquisition of knowledge is essential for human beings. All through life a human needs to continually gain knowledge to survive, to evolve and to reach the ultimate state of Enlightenment. And knowledge falls under two main categories. One is gathering external facts and figures, a general or specific information required for making a living. The other is exploring the deeper recesses of one's personality until the true Self is revealed.

All educational institutions, schools and universities provide you the knowledge of the world. It is objective knowledge pertaining to the terrestrial realm. As you keep on acquiring this knowledge it will increase in degree but not improve in kind. It will not help you gain subjective knowledge of the Self within. The Knowledge of Self is of a different kind which reveals the transcendental Reality.

Objective knowledge operates within the limits of this world. It cannot reach the supreme Self within. Just as the knowledge of the dreamer is confined to the dream world. However brilliant a dreamer be, his knowledge cannot reach the waker and the waking world. The knowledge of the dream and waking are of different kinds. So also are the knowledge of the waking world and that of Self. All the objective knowledge gained by the waker cannot attain Self-knowledge, spiritual Enlightenment.

Ignorance of Self keeps you in spiritual darkness. And all through life you are persecuted by trials and tribulations, worries and anxieties. The solution to all your problems lies in gaining knowledge of the inner Self. Imagine a person moving around in the darkness of a room. He will strike against cornices and corners, obstacles and obstructions and hurt himself. To save himself from breakage and damage he must bring in light. There is no other way to it. So too, any amount of objective knowledge cannot liberate you from the endless persecution of the ever changing world. You need the subjective knowledge of Self to provide you with enduring peace and bliss.

Love

Love is identification with fellow beings. Realising your oneness with others. Feeling peaceful with one and all. With love you find harmony with the world around you. Those who lack love develop preferential attachment to particular persons and fall out of harmony with the rest.

To be successful in any field of activity you need the feeling of love to create a spirit of cooperative endeavour among your colleagues. With a team spirit thus created your organisation would flourish. You can apply the same principle effectively in all facets of your life. It takes you on the path of success and progress.

Power

Where there is an attitude of unselfishness, a spirit of service and sacrifice there would be power, strength in that person or organisation. Whereas, a selfish attitude drains one's power and strength. A truth that is hardly known. Consequently, people are self-centred, selfish only to lose their energy and potency in action.

Selfishness is a trait a person develops when he functions in the world only to benefit himself at the expense of others. Ironically, a human being alone can work in his field with a spirit of service and sacrifice. By fixing an ideal at work beyond a self-centred interest. The ideal that he sets may be for the growth and progress of his company, community or country. The higher the ideal the greater would be his initiative to work. And greater the power and strength in action.

CHAPTER VI

WORK ETHICS FOR
EFFECTIVE MANAGEMENT

An organisation with all the inputs for effective management could still break down if it lacks character. The members of the organisation, particularly the chief executive, must conduct the business with ethics and morality. An institution run without sound character and conduct would be rendered spineless. Nevertheless, there is little awareness or discussion on this vital subject in management lobbies. As a result business executives have become licentious, greedy and they exploit others. The modern business houses stand out in metropolises as magnificent edifices lacking adequate ethical foundation. Sooner or later they are bound to collapse. History has proved it. Yet the blunder continues defying detection, much less correction.

Ego

The virus that attacks the character of human beings is one's ego and egocentric desires. The ego is an exhibition, overemphasis of one's person. An exaggerated projection of oneself over others. The 'I' that wants to get bigger and bigger. Craves to be known and idolised. In the process one develops insatiable desires to maintain and inflate the ego. Most of these desires remain unfulfilled to cause mental agitation, frustration, stress.

Ego manifests in a person in three distinct ways:

1. I am supreme
2. I alone exist
3. I am the doer.

In the first manifestation of ego the person considers himself supreme. Feels intoxicated with an air of superiority. Suffers from a superiority complex. With pride and vanity he puts himself on a higher pedestal and regards others inferior to him. Thus estranging himself from his colleagues. You must be careful you do not develop this noxious trait. It segregates you from the rest and ruins the spirit of cooperative endeavour in the organisation.

In the second manifestation he feels himself all-important. As though he alone exists. And everybody and everything is meant to cater to his person. Totally self-centred, his interest and conduct is directed to his wellbeing at the expense of others.

A third way, the ego manifests as the notion of doership: I am the doer, I do everything. A sense of arrogating every piece of work done to one's sole effort, none else. Such a person fails to recognise the contributions of many others towards his achievement. Without which it would not have been possible for him to accomplish it. Take an example of the designer of the latest model of the Mercedes Benz. No doubt he has produced an excellent car. But he must realise that thousands of varied technicians have contributed their expertise in the past and present towards its creation. To ignore all their inputs and arrogate the new model to his sole effort is the play of the ego. His 'I' sticks out more than his work.

Ego is deadly. It creates waves of disparity and disharmony in the society. The foolish are victimised by their own ego. You must ensure you do not fall a prey to it. Learn to look at the world dispassionately. Not egoistically. Try to understand how nature works. How the animate and the inanimate are knit together to form the universe. How all of them act as spokes in the wheel of life. Each one playing a distinct part. So must you play your part. He that is ignorant of this phenomenon does not perceive the great plan of nature. Fails to look at himself as a part of the whole. Develops the petty ego and suffers.

You must get wiser than that. Understand that everyone in this wide world possesses a talent of his own. And you are one such. Why do you have to compare yourself with others. Just play your life's role without an air of superiority or inferiority. Live your life in a spirit of dispassion. Remember, all the world is a stage and all men and women mere actors playing their different roles. The great American philosopher-poet, Ralph Waldo Emerson drives home this thought in his simple poem: *The Mountain and the Squirrel*. The poem narrates a quarrel between the mountain and the squirrel. The mountain brags of its stature and strength. That it carries forests on its back. And disparages the little squirrel. The squirrel accepts it cannot carry forests on its back but challenges the mountain to crack a nut! So it is with the world. None important, none unimportant. The poem:

The Mountain and the Squirrel

The mountain and the squirrel
Had a quarrel;
And the former called the latter "Little Prig."
Bun replied,
"You are doubtless very big;
But all sorts of things and weather
Must be taken in together,
To make up a year
And a sphere.
And I think it no disgrace
To occupy my place.
If I'm not so large as you,
You are not so small as I,
And not half so spry,
I'll not deny you make
A very pretty squirrel track;
Talents differ; all is well and wisely put;
If I cannot carry forests on my back,
Neither can you crack a nut."

— Ralph Waldo Emerson

Egocentric Desires

The ego further generates a plethora of desires which go through several modifications. When a *desire* is intercepted by any form of obstruction it metamorphoses into *anger*. You become angry at the interruption. And when your desires are fed, you develop *greed* for gaining more. If your greed too is fulfilled and you get all that you wanted, you entertain *fear* of losing it. Or develop *arrogance* at those that have less than you, *envy* at those that have more.

Most human beings are trapped in a quagmire of emotions. And their thinking is affected; their actions lose direction and power. As a result the businesses run by them ultimately collapse. A debacle that has been repeated for long the world over. Yet there has been no attempt to decipher the cause of it. It eludes the grasp of businesspersons, their schools and institutions. They fail to realise their limitation in handling this inherent problem. It all ends in upsetting the economies of countries.

You must realise the play of ego and desire affects your mental equanimity and work. You therefore cannot afford to let loose your ego and develop indiscriminate desires. Desire no doubt is an inherent part of action. There can be no action without a desire preceding it. But the gush of desires has to be monitored, directed with a sound intellect. Your intellect must remain ever in control over the mind's emotional demands and channelise actions through proper judgement and decision. That is self-management. And self-management is the sap that runs through all healthy business management.

Having thus controlled your ego and egocentric desires, the intellect must set proper work ethics for effective management in your field of activity. That would create the initiative within to work diligently without having to depend on external stimuli from incentives. And provide the real thrust to productivity and progress in business. Bereft of management ethics business executives are victimised by oppressive desires and bludgeoned by heavy borrowing well beyond their means. They may bloom for a while only to pale and perish. For enduring success therefore businesspersons must refrain from indiscriminate borrowing. And structure themselves with sound principles of character and conduct. To achieve this some of the ethical values are enumerated herein for grafting them into regular business practice.

Work Ethics

Effective management requires personnel with ethical and moral values ingrained in them. These values are founded on selflessness. An unselfish approach would require a high and noble ideal to follow. Such an ideal is based on service and sacrifice at the physical level, feeling of love and friendship at the emotional level and thought of a charitable disposition and accommodation at the intellectual level.

Service: Physical Level

The foremost value in business culture is service-centredness as opposed to self-centredness. But corporate executives run their business primarily to feed their ego and personal desires. The general attitude prevailing in business is gross self-centredness. 'What can I get out of my company' is the chorus sung in corporate circles the world over. The thought of customer service has become a gimmick. And community service has been long lost. The culture of giving, sharing has yielded to the desire, greed of taking, aggrandising. The tsunami of greed in humans has swallowed up giant corporations and companies causing financial crashes round the world.

Human beings would do well to learn the art of sharing, giving, serving. This fine trait creates the right mental climate at work. Which is most conducive for better production and growth in business. Your motto in life therefore should be to strive, to struggle and not merely crave for success. Never care for the result of action. You run after success, it eludes you. Leave it alone, it follows you. It is a law of nature.

Love: Emotional Level

Another ethical value is entertaining a feeling of love, friendship, camaraderie. A sense of belonging through identification with others. Sharing of emotions. Empathising with colleagues at work. The atmosphere in a business house should have a feeling of fraternity for it to flourish. The lack of love and friendship causes an air of indifference among colleagues. Spoils the spirit of cooperative endeavour essential for success and progress in any establishment.

The feeling of love arises with the right understanding and relationship. An organisation is made up of different types of people, each working with his particular expertise. From a broader perspective management provides finance and knowhow while labour executes, manufactures the products. And under these two divisions there are several layers of personnel pouring out their individual faculties to make up the total workforce. All of them act as spokes to the corporate wheel. Each member must understand this natural setup and develop the feeling of oneness. That is identification, love. Without the backing of such emotion there would be disruptions and disputes ruining the growth of the organisation.

Charitable Disposition: Intellectual Level

A business organisation is constituted of manifold categories of employees with a wide range of individual calibre. Possessing varied talent and capability. However, everyone in the company cannot work at the highest level of competence and efficiency. The chief executive must clearly understand this as a matter of fact. He must look at work performed by each of them objectively. Not pushing them beyond their optimum capacity. Have a charitable disposition to accept each one's service at the level of one's competence. That does not mean that a CEO should tolerate lethargy and indifference in his workforce. His intellect must visualise each one's capacity to function while he helps them all grow in the organisation. He is soft but firm in the execution of his duty and responsibility.

Another important aspect of management is to encourage free exchange of ideas. Appreciate others' point of view. It would not only be unethical but unproductive to egoistically hang on to one's own way of functioning. Your intellect must check your ego to be able to examine others' thoughts and opinions and learn to accept them when it admits reason and logic.

One may possess character and conduct one's business with proper work ethics and yet face grave problems with the world around. Since the world is infested with evil and corrupt ways of functioning. How then does one encounter these problems and deal with corruption.

Deal with Corruption

Corruption is a human weakness rampant everywhere. It has become a part of human life. However, humans are privileged to deal with it appropriately. They should learn the fine art of relating to corruption properly instead of merely grumbling, complaining about it. Having mastered the art you enjoy meeting and overcoming these challenges of life like a sportsman does with his opposition. Management then becomes one big game of life, no burden.

Corruption may be defined as wicked, sinful living bereft of ethics and morality. A life of iniquity fed by falsehood, bribery and other unlawful practices. You must first realise that corruption has existed from time immemorial. Good and evil has ever remained an inherent part of the world. The scriptures speak about it as god and the devil. The English poet John Milton in his legendary poem *Paradise Lost* writes about the gods and demons. The great Indian epic *Mahabharata* narrates the battle between two royal families, the virtuous Pandavas and the vicious Kauravas depicting the perennial conflict between good and evil. The wise have indicated that corruption cannot quite be eradicated from the world. Any attempt to do so tantamounts to straightening a dog's tail. You need not be unduly perturbed while you ensure that you are not a part of it. Jesus Christ has cautioned humanity in unequivocal terms: *Iniquity there shall be in this world; woe unto you if you be the cause of it.*

Therefore use your intellect to rise above this immoral trait and treat it appropriately. To begin with learn to view corruption from a higher level of wisdom and maturity. Look at corrupt practices among people as you would view the innocent selfishness in children. Children could be very selfish and possessive with their petty toys and trinkets. They even play false and cheat other children to hoard their trivial possessions. But you as an adult understand their pettiness, their childish innocence. And know they would soon grow out of their childishness. Similarly, your intellect must understand the small minds, petty desires and silly practices of corrupt people. Sympathise with their ignorance and the lack of perception of higher values of life. Look at their behaviour as a play of spiritual infancy. And help them wherever possible to rise to a saner life of moral values. With such a mature attitude of sympathetic understanding your mind would remain calm and composed. And your intellect clear and sharp to handle corruption with strength and confidence.

The Belgian Nobel laureate in literature, Maurice Maeterlinck presents this philosophic view of life in a striking message to humanity: *Happy and blessed hour, when wickedness stands forth revealed as goodness bereft of its guide.* You reach a happy state when you look at a corrupt person as one deprived of education on the right values. Everyone therefore is inherently good. The good turns into bad when ethical and moral values are not instilled in them from the very beginning. This insight helps you develop a positive and practical approach to life.

The Aggressive and the Passive

The general grievance everywhere is that the innocent suffer at the hands of the vicious. That the honest are deceived and harassed while the dishonest exploit and prosper. The innocent are frustrated not knowing the reason for this paradox in life. The reason becomes obvious with a study of the inner personality of humans. A careful analysis would reveal that the nature of human beings falls under two broad classifications. The *aggressive* and the *passive*. Each of these can further be classified as good and bad. Thus there are the aggressive good and aggressive bad persons. Likewise, the passive good and passive bad. As illustrated below:

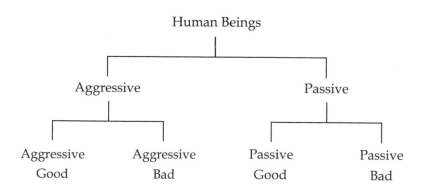

The terms *aggressive* and *passive* herein have a particular connotation depending on the use or non use of the intellect respectively. The mind and intellect are the two equipments that propel human activity. The physical body cannot act on its own. Actions proceed either from the mind or the intellect. A person would be classified as *passive* when he acts from feeling and emotion of the mind without the guidance of the intellect. Whereas, he who acts with the intellect governing the mind through reason and judgement would be classified as *aggressive*.

A passive person functioning from his mind's feeling and emotion may be good or bad. He conducts himself either way unaware of his goodness or badness. He merely manifests his good or bad impulses. His intellect is not sufficiently developed to examine the nature of his activities. He does not intend to be either good or bad. Thus there are passively good and passively bad persons.

In contrast to the passive, the aggressive function with the intellect. The aggressive also may be categorised as good or bad. An aggressively bad person is wilfully vicious, catering to his personal interests. He plans and schemes, manipulates and manoeuvres in his immoral, corrupt way of living. Breaks customs and traditions, rules and regulations to feed his egocentric desires. The use of the intellect makes him more powerful to dominate over the passive good and bad. Since the passive do not use the intellect and function directly from the mind they succumb to the oppression of the aggressive bad. As opposed to the aggressive bad, the aggressive good is essentially benevolent. He uses his intellect to evaluate his role in life and act in the best interest of the community at large. He is charitably disposed, service oriented.

Study these four classifications of human nature. You will find that the honest suffer because of lack of use of the intellect. Operating at the level of the mind the passive become victims of intellectual manipulations of the aggressive bad. The solution to this problem lies in the passive developing and using their intellect to turn into aggressive good persons. The aggressive bad dread the aggressive good. Aggressive goodness would therefore take care of all evil and corruption in the world. Not knowing this solution there is no attempt to develop, strengthen the intellect and promote aggressive goodness. Instead, people lead a passive life, complain of malpractices and suffer at the hands of the oppressors.

The development of the intellect however would need time and effort. As you develop the intellect to set right the malpractices you must also try to take a mature stand and sympathise with the ignorance and foolish behaviour of the wicked. Understand the world as an admixture of good and evil. Neither virtue nor vice can sustain itself indefinitely. The good yields to the bad. So does bad to good. The cycle rolls on perennially. People are caught up in this cycle. They become elated with the good, dejected with the bad. But a human being is designed not to be affected by these fluctuations. Keep his mind calm and composed in and through life's changes. A calm mind helps the intellect become sharp to effectively manage one's affairs in life.

CHAPTER VII

PRINCIPLES OF STRESS MANAGEMENT

It is no pessimism to state that the present-day world is infested with stress everywhere. With all the spectacular advancement of science and technology people are beset with trial and tribulation, worry and anxiety, sorrow and suffering in life. The bouts of pleasure and joy which they claim in their passage through life are but streaks of lightning in the darkness of distress. Nevertheless, there is little scientific investigation of this grave problem that humanity faces.

The psychiatrists have not indeed probed into the true cause of stress. They have merely fixed labels of diseases to it. And all the while the treatment has been from the wrong end. External and not internal. They treat the effect rather than the cause. The plague continues to take its toll on human lives. None seems to be concerned, much less interested in investigating its primary cause. Consequently, stress has assumed epidemic proportions while pharmacists thrive with their competitive antidepressant drugs.

Another abuse of authority in dealing with this problem is the stress management courses conducted by distressed management consultants. With no clue to the origin of stress. They suggest methods of combating stress without actually grappling with the problem. And offer cosmetic solutions which may provide some temporary relief to those who attend their courses. But none of them is directed to eradicate this mental illness from the mass of humanity.

The above treatment of stress is least addressed to the inherent problem. Stress is wrongly attributed to external factors. Like those inflicted with stress complain of a hysterical husband or a nagging wife. Others grumble at the exorbitant demands of labour or exploitation by management. Yet others fuss over summer being hot or winter being cold. People throughout the world live with the belief that factors outside themselves produce stress. Hence, to combat it the focus of attention and correction has been directed to outer forces. None realises that stress is caused internally. And any form of external treatment is futile. The problem therefore remains unsolved and human minds are consumed by stress. The real solution to this perennial problem is to find its source. Whence does it emanate? Unless the origin is located and dealt with one cannot free oneself from stress. Ironically, there is no attempt to identify its root. Well-meaning therapists shear its shoots only to find them emerging again and again.

Consider for example there is a foul odour in your lounge. You try to remove the smell by spraying air fresheners and perfumes. The spraying may help drown the smell for a while only for it to reappear. It will persist unless its origin is identified and treated. After a careful examination you do find its source. The smell is emanating from a decomposed mouse lying behind the curtain. Having located it you would know exactly how to get rid of that foul odour. So it is with stress. Those who claim to have solutions for stress deal with it superficially. The root remains unattended while fresh shoots emerge to leave the therapist and sufferer bewildered.

Anatomy of Stress

To get to the source of stress the inner personality has to be examined. A human being is constituted of the body, mind and intellect. The physical body houses the mind and intellect. Hence a clear understanding of these inner equipments and their functioning is of prime importance.

The mind comprises impulses, feelings, emotions, likes and dislikes. The intellect is that which thinks, reasons, judges, decides. When the mind propels an action without the intellect's guidance, then the action is said to be impulsive. When the intellect guides the mind in action, the action is considered intellectual. If however the intellect is weak it loses control over the mind. The mind then develops endless desires and produces desire-ridden, impulsive actions. Which results in mental agitation, stress.

The human mind thus left uncontrolled by the intellect can distress a person. The mind behaves like a child. The nature of a child is ever impulsive, heedless and irresponsible. It needs constant supervision and guidance of an adult. So does your mind need the attention and direction of the intellect. Most people succumb to the indiscriminate pressures of the mind. Their life is riddled with stress. And they suffer the consequences thereof.

Mind Wreaks Havoc

Herein are some of the attributes of the mind which determine its character:

1. The mind is replete with likes and dislikes, attractions and aversions

2. Has a natural tendency to ramble into the past or the future

3. Generates endless desires

4. Develops attachment, possessiveness to objects and beings.

When these qualities of the mind are not supervised by the intellect they can cause stress and strain through one's life. And with the complete loss of control the mind could prove detrimental, even fatal.

Likes and Dislikes

The human mind is constituted of one's likes and dislikes. People are enmeshed in their attractions and aversions. It all starts from early childhood. From the very beginning you tend to pick what you like and discard what you do not like. Besides you collecting them, your well-wishers, parents and later in life your spouse and children constantly feed your likes and dislikes. Following this behavioural pattern right through life you are left with a stockpile of distinct likes and dislikes. Which now acts like a motor driving you to do what you like and avoid what you dislike. In effect it determines your lifestyle which moves on fixed rails. The rigidity in movement causes your life to traverse through rough terrain, sometimes resulting in a crash.

You must realise the world is ever in a flux of change. It cannot cater to your personal likes and dislikes at all times. You like summer and not the other three seasons. But the seasons must roll by. That provides you three months of satisfaction and leaves you dissatisfied the other nine months. Again, you like to have a glass of alcohol after a tiring day at work. But your partner at home frowns at the idea of consuming alcohol. Her behaviour frustrates you. The list is endless. All these contribute to your stress.

There is yet another grave problem in indiscriminately pursuing your likes and spurning your dislikes. The problem stems from a strange paradox in human life.

Which misguides the mass of humanity to virtually court suffering. The paradox is that the experiences which are pleasurable in the beginning turn out to be detrimental towards the end and what is detestable in the beginning becomes beneficial, even enjoyable in the end. It is the irony of life that sorrow appears in the garb of joy and joy in the garb of sorrow. Should nature present pleasure and pain, joy and sorrow in their true perspective humanity would be free from the problem of stress.

Unaware of the paradox human beings mechanically yield to pleasant beginnings only to end in bitterness. Also avoid unpleasant beginnings and lose the joy of life later. To cite a few examples, people like to laze and dislike physical exercise. Like to eat junk food and dislike health food. Prefer to sleep late and wake up late. Detest to go to bed early and rise early. The tendency is to grab instant pleasures and suffer the consequential sorrows. Few go through the initial displeasure and enjoy the benefit accruing therefrom.

The trouble with most people is that they fall an easy prey to their likes and dislikes. Even cultivate more in the course of their life. And end up in greater frustration. Likes and dislikes are no doubt an inherent part of your life. There is nothing fundamentally wrong with them. You need not avoid them. Only ensure that your likes and dislikes do not directly drive your activities. By using reason and judgement of your intellect not to be enticed by instant pleasures or be put off by initial displeasures. Thus must you programme them properly towards what is beneficial for your growth, progress and evolution.

Ramblings of the Mind

The human mind has the awkward tendency of slipping into past memories or future imaginations. An ungoverned mind goes on worrying over the past or gets anxious for the future. The mind thus becomes agitated unless the intellect controls the ramblings and keeps it calm.

Worry and anxiety saps one's energy, causes fatigue. But you believe that work tires you. Work can never tire you. What actually causes fatigue is your worry of the past and anxiety for the future. To handle that you need cups of coffee to stimulate you at work. A few pegs of alcohol to recreate you at the end of the day. After five days' work you must have the weekend break. Thank God It's Friday! And you eagerly wait for the end of the year for your vacation. With all these breaks you still feel fatigued, stressed.

Ironically no child is ever fatigued. Unlike the adult. Though children are weak and adults strong. The young are always bristling with activity, effervescing with joy. While the older ones have lost their energy. The reason is simple. Children have no worry of the past or anxiety for the future. While adults are infested with worry and anxiety. You need to learn this lesson from infants. Use your intellect to free yourself from the pressures of the past and future and focus your attention on the present. That should save the energy to function stressless in life.

Endless Desires

A human being is replete with desires. His uncontrolled mind generates endless desires. The mind is compared to fire. You may feed fire with logs and logs of wood. It consumes them all and is ready for more. Likewise, the mind is insatiable. Always eager to consume more and more objects of desires. With the endless generation of desires the bulk of them remain unfulfilled. The unfulfilled desires cause mental agitation. And stress is mental agitation produced by unfulfilled desires.

Besides multiplying in numbers, the desires in your mind go through various modifications producing different kinds of emotions. When your *desire* is fed it grows into *greed, avarice.* And when the desire, greed is fulfilled and you have gained what you wanted you develop *fear.* You are afraid of losing what you have gained. On the contrary if your desire is obstructed, intercepted by an object or being it turns into *anger.* To cite a simple example, Tom loves Elizabeth. Tom has a desire to possess and enjoy her company. Another suitor, John intercepts his desire. Tom develops *anger* towards John. Again, when desire, greed or anger wells up your mind whirls into *delusion.* When your emotions reach that stage you develop *arrogance* at those below your level of achievement and *envy* at those above your level. Thus a host of emotions invades your personality.

Desires multiply like bacteria. Unfulfilled desires along with their modifications produce stress. You need to use your intellect to constantly monitor your desires. If you fail to do so and leave them unattended your life would remain stressful.

You may wonder how one could operate, conduct any business without a free flow of desires. Modern management clearly encourages business executives to step up their desires. Also, the fact remains that desire precedes action. There can be no action without it. Nevertheless, it is not in your interest to let your desires operate on their own. Since they have no direction or dimension. They need to be guided, directed by the intellect. When properly governed, monitored by the intellect they assume the form of an aim, aspiration or ambition. And that would lead executives to achievement and success in business. However, the world today lacks the application of the intellect and ungoverned desires, besides causing stress, are virtually destroying business houses.

An important note of caution needs to be observed while you pursue your desires. You may achieve the objects of your desires and enjoy them. Only ensure that your present happiness is not dependent on your future achievements. Let your mind be content with what you possess while your intellect aspires to gain more. Your mind would then be peaceful at all times. A calm mind would render your intellect sharp to fulfil your desires. On the contrary, if you do not heed this note of caution your mind would always be hanging on your unfulfilled future. Hence, your present state all through life would remain disturbed, smitten with stress. Resulting in loss of direction and productivity in action.

Attachment and Possessiveness

Another dreadful quality of the mind is its attachment to the objects and beings of the world. Attachment is a pernicious passion destroying the peace and harmony of human beings. People all over the world suffer from attachment which passes off as love. A boy meets a girl and gets attached to her. He raises a family and develops attachment for the family. Procures a house and becomes attached to it. Starts a business, earns money and is attached to his wealth. Another, tired of material pursuits, joins a service club like the Rotary. And gets attached to the club. The mind thus, lacking the guidance of the intellect, binds itself to practically anything it contacts. This mental bondage is attachment. It has devastated the human race with sorrow and suffering.

Attachment and possessiveness are two sides of a coin. When a person is attached to an object or being he becomes possessive towards it. The virus of 'my' and 'mine' infects the relation between them. And the relation suffers, ultimately breaks. He loses the object or being of his attachment. People are not aware of this stern reality. Even the intelligentsia are victims of the deadly trait of attachment and possessiveness.

And the entire human race continues to suffer through confrontation and conflict, separation and divorce. Yet few realise that one develops one's own attachment and causes the consequent misery.

The trait of attachment and possessiveness runs through the life of humans. From early childhood to ripe old age. A child is attached to its playthings, its dollies and pollies, its toys and trinkets. And develops possessiveness towards them. Consequently, it is disturbed by the gain or loss of its possessions. When the child grows up into an adult, he is attached to his partner, wealth, name, fame etc. And develops possessiveness towards them. He is disturbed, harassed by the fluctuations of their gain and loss.

Attachment is actually a pollution of love. When love is vitiated by self-centredness, selfishness it turns sour, changes to attachment. Vice versa. When attachment drops its self-centred motives it becomes love.

Love   + Selfishness = Attachment
Attachment − Selfishness = Love

To avoid this self-inflicted damage to your personality you need a powerful intellect to protect, preserve your love. Ensure the purity of your love is not marred by self-centred motives. Remember, love generates peace and harmony unlike attachment which causes distress and disharmony.

When a person is riddled with attachments his life would be stressful. Besides being stressed, he would be estranged from that object or person of attachment. Sooner or later each other's relationship will be lost. Either of them would desert the other. Even perish at times. And leave the lover in distress. It is a law of nature.

Assess the World

The mind therefore is the source of stress. And the intellect alone can control the vagaries of the mind to bring about your peace and happiness. But this exercise involves the development of the intellect. Your intellect must reach a position of strength to be able to manage the persistent demands of the mind. Which requires your effort for a length of time. A weak intellect cannot be strengthened overnight. Meanwhile your mind will continue to exert stress. Hence you would need some form of interim relief before you are able to fortify the intellect to govern the mind. The practical way to find that relief is for you to assess the world around properly and establish the right relation with object or being, environment or situation you encounter in life.

It is of prime importance that you make a proper assessment of the world around you. Especially the people in close contact with you. Your partner, your kids, your colleagues at work etc. Likewise, you must examine and assess the environment, situation, weather, everything you meet in daily life. If you assess the world thus, you would know exactly what to expect of it. If you do not assess or make a wrong assessment, you would then entertain unreasonable hopes and expectations from it. You would want the world to fit into your frame of mind. That causes disappointment and stress in your life. But when your assessment is proper you would not have unreasonable hopes and expectations. No disappointments. Your life then would run smooth. Free from stress. A wife will not grumble of her husband consuming alcohol. Nor a husband complain of his nagging wife.

People all over the world fail to understand that every human being is distinct and different from another. That each is governed by one's own singular nature. Therefore you must assess the nature of each human individually. But hardly anyone follows this practice in life. Without making individual assessment you would not be able to relate to others properly. As a result you expect one to behave different from one's fundamental nature. How can you expect a hysterical boss to conduct himself in a calm and composed manner at office? How can you expect a nagging wife to be understanding and accommodating at home? How can you expect bubbling teenagers to be mature and objective? Since you fail to assess their individual characters you find them all faulty in their behaviour. You attribute these 'faults' to those who helplessly express their inner nature. You do not realise that you err in expecting them to conduct themselves different from their basic quality and character. You expect the impossible. Your erroneous hopes and expectations cause you stress. You must understand that people are constrained to live their own lives. You may try and correct a person or situation, but what cannot be cured has to be endured. Remember, all grumbling tantamounts to, "Oh! Why is a lily not an oak?"

Interestingly, the problem of assessment of living beings relates to humans alone and not to any other creature. With respect to other creatures you understand that each species behaves according to its collective nature. That all lions are fierce and ferocious and all deer are meek and mild. Which makes it easy for you to assess each animal since it has the collective nature of its species. And not a separate nature of its own as a human does. Hence your relation with all creatures except human is perfect. You would feed a deer in a zoo but keep your distance from a lion's cage. You would pick up a kitten and fondle it but admire a cobra from afar. Right assessment. No wrong expectation. No disappointment. No stress.

Assessment does not stop with living creatures alone. You need to assess the nature of the country you live in, community you associate with, company you work for, weather at your place etc. A typical example of a lack of or wrong assessment is a common complaint about the weather. Every morning people are either elated over its brightness or depressed by its dullness. The fluctuations of the weather should affect the weather vanes, not humans. Yet people turn schizophrenic over the natural changes in weather. You would complain of cold during winter, heat in summer or wetness all through the monsoon. Your grumbling never ends. When something goes wrong in the external world and can be corrected, you may do so. If however it is not possible to correct it you must learn to live with it. If you do not, you would feel disappointed, stressed. You cause your own stress.

A true episode that took place in Chennai, India in 1939 drives home this point. It was a humid day in summer and the temperature shot up to 44 degrees Celsius. The students in the classroom were all fussing about the sweltering heat. The master noticed their fuss as he entered the classroom. He walked past his desk to the other side into an open quadrangle and beckoned the students to come out. He stood under the blazing noonday sun. As the students wondered at what was happening he threw up his arms and exclaimed, "Boys, isn't this a beautiful summer?" The boys could not relate to what he said. He continued, "The beauty of the summer is its scorching heat. The beauty of the winter is its biting cold. The beauty of the monsoon is its persistent showers. But the problem with you all is that you want the summer to be cold, the winter to be warm, the monsoon to be dry!" The wise man did not stop at that. He exemplified further, "The beauty of the African is his dark skin. The beauty of the Englishman is his fair skin. But the African wants to be fair. The Englishman wants to be tanned." The madness goes on and on. You would be totally unreasonable in expecting object and being, environment and situation of the world to be different from their fundamental nature. Since they do not fit into your mental pattern you remain frustrated through life.

Therefore, learn to look at persons, beings and things, environments and situations as they are and not what you would like them to be. You would then begin to appreciate the wondrous phenomenon of nature. And admire the beauty of temper in your husband and the art of nagging in your wife! You thus become free from stress.

Remember the words of wisdom pronounced by the American poet Oliver Wendell Holmes Sr.:

> *For him in vain the envious seasons roll*
> *Who bears eternal summer in his soul.*

CHAPTER VIII

SCIENCE OF PRODUCTIVITY

The mind and intellect together constitute your inner personality which is housed in your physical body. Productivity in any field of activity requires a sharp intellect and a calm mind. When the mind is disturbed with many unfulfilled desires and consequent worries and anxieties, the intellect loses its focus and application to work. The intellect needs to be strengthened to maintain the mind's focus in the wake of its desires and demands. And the intellect exercising its control over the mind is self-management. No external management would be effective until you are self-managed. Which in effect means that your actions are propelled by the intellect and not directly by the mind. Hence you need to build a strong intellect and keep the mind composed to optimise production in your field of activity.

The physical body no doubt executes actions. But the body per se cannot act. My body cannot write these lines on its own. Neither can your body sit down and read these lines. There is something other than the body which drives it to act. It is either the mind or the intellect. If the actions are propelled by the mind alone they would be emotional, impulsive. If controlled and guided by the intellect then those actions would be intellectual, discretionary. An executive working in a corporation may possess adequate educational qualification and technical training but his productivity will be impaired if he acts impulsively, not intellectually. Ironically, executives in business houses are selected with great care on the basis of their academic achievements rather than their intellectual strength. Consequently, the academics with undeveloped intellect have caused the repeated downfall of corporations.

Objectivity in Action

A human has to play several roles in his life. As a citizen of his country. A manager in his office. Parent of his family. Secretary of his club. And several others. It is interesting to examine what happens to the manifold roles while an individual plays a particular role. When he is on the role of a manager at office how does he deal with the rest of them? Does he ignore or remember them all? If he carries the memory of his other roles while performing his present action it would interfere with his concentration. If on the contrary he forgets them completely, his present action may offend his obligation to another role. For example, a manager cannot afford to forget that he is a foreign citizen while executing his action in a country other than his own. Either way, remembering or forgetting other obligations at any time could cause a problem. The solution lies in being generally aware of other roles without allowing them to intrude upon the present action. You should keep them in the background and not let their memory interfere with whatever you are engaged in at any time. That is being objective. Your intellect does not allow other thoughts in the mind disturb the concentration and execution of your present activity. Maintaining objectivity is an essential requirement of an executive to optimise productivity in his actions.

A common problem that harasses the corporate world is the lack of objectivity. Businesspersons and professionals carry family problems to their offices and official problems to their homes. They are unable to switch off domestic concerns while at office or official concerns at home. And focus on their present occupation. That impairs efficiency, productivity both in their office and home. The human mind thus tends to slip into other attachments and fails to pursue a disciplined course of action to achieve its goal. And loses its focus of attention, objectivity in action. Resulting in the loss of production.

Gain Objectivity

The process of developing objectivity falls under two heads:

1. Building a strong intellect
2. Pursuing an ideal in life.

Building the *intellect* is not the same as gaining *intelligence.* You gain intelligence by acquiring information, knowledge from external sources. From teachers and textbooks, schools and universities and other educational institutions. You use these sources to become well-informed, knowledgeable, even brilliant in the subject you pursue. The intelligence thus acquired provides you the means to make a living. You go through a medical school to gain the knowledge of medicine. An engineering school to gain the knowledge of engineering. Etcetera. All these knowledges help you earn to live in the world.

The *intellect* is fundamentally different from *intelligence*. Any amount of intelligence acquired cannot per se build your intellect. The intelligence you gain is much like data fed into a computer. All the knowledge stored in a computer is of no use to it. Likewise, you cannot use the knowledge gained without the intellect. The stronger the intellect the greater would be your ability to use the knowledge acquired in life.

To build the intellect you must question, think, reason all through your life. Never take anything for granted. Accept only those that admit logic and reason. By building a powerful intellect you will be able to use whatever intelligence you possess. Mere intelligence without the intellect to apply it tantamounts to gold bars loaded on a mule's back. Yet people do not care to develop this life-saving, life-sustaining equipment, the intellect. Galileo Galilei, the father of modern astronomy, wondered how humans could ignore the use of their intellect: *I do not feel obliged to believe that the same God who has endowed us with sense, reason and intellect has intended us to forego their use.*

The second part in the process of developing objectivity is to set an ideal to work for. Examine your motive in action. What is it you are working for? Is your interest confined only to the welfare of yourself and your immediate family? Or does your interest go beyond the precinct of your family to cover your company or community? Or stretch even further to embrace the interest of your nation or of all human beings? The larger the circle of your dedication to serve and sacrifice, the greater the cause you work for, the higher is your ideal. In fixing your ideal in life ensure that it is realistic depending upon your present nature and capacity. Of course, your ideal could be increased later as your capacity grows to a higher level of dedication. Keeping your ideal firm, your intellect must channelise your actions towards achieving it. Pursue the ideal set until you reach it.

While pursuing the ideal your mind could slip into other attractions. And your actions digress towards the mind's attractions. You then lose your objectivity. Hence the intellect must constantly monitor the mind's transgressions and ensure that your actions are directed to the set ideal. That is being objective in action. As your intellect maintains objectivity you optimise productivity in business.

Initiative versus Incentive

The intellect plays a vital role in your business. It serves to fix an ideal beyond your self-centred interest and direct your actions towards achieving it. When you thus conduct your business objectively for a higher cause you develop the *initiative* within to work. An *initiative* drives one to work tirelessly with enthusiasm and cheer. Whereas a person with no such ideal in life works with ego and egocentric desires merely to satisfy his selfish interests. Such a person would have no *initiative* to work. And with a lack of *initiative* his work turns burdensome. He becomes tired and fatigued. At times incapacitated to work. He would need regular breaks for weekends and vacations to recuperate and return to work. Not realising what has gone wrong, management bodies worldwide have desperately devised the whip of *incentives* to boost work output. Which has resulted in the decline of business acumen and productivity.

The need of the hour is to carefully study, analyse the difference between *initiative* and *incentive* and how they relate to work. Work performed with an unselfish ideal for a higher cause is natural, organic. It generates the *initiative* to inspire workers to perform effortlessly. And those who adopt this spirit of service would continue to act tirelessly without the need for external stimulants. Such work backed by an *initiative* produces a long-term benefit. And their work output would rise to the optimum.

On the contrary, work undertaken with selfish motive and no ideal is tiring, fatiguing. It lacks lustre. It would need external stimulants to activate the workers. Modern business houses are doing just that. Constantly boosting the workforce with *incentives* for personal reward. *Incentives*, such as increased emoluments or perks, no doubt give an initial thrust to work but they have a diminishing value. Ultimately, the workers become neutralised to enhanced pay or perk. The *incentives* which initially stimulated them lose their power to generate work any more. Which has led to loss of productivity.

Besides, *incentives* for personal rewards create discontent and disharmony among the members of a corporation. Conversely, those functioning with *initiative* generate peace and harmony to better their performance.

For generations people have been misled to seek rewards for their work. They desire short-term gains, quick-fixes. Rare indeed are those who would want to put in adequate effort to achieve their goal. You must learn to deserve and not merely desire the fruit of your actions. Little do people realise the beauty and grandeur of *karma* – action, service and sacrifice. Instead, the general trend the world over is to employ inorganic means to gain their end results. Thus sprang the liberal use of fertilizers in different facets of life for a synthetic, unreal growth. *Incentives* used freely to promote business act in much the same way as fertilizers.

The modern agriculturists use chemicals to fertilize, boost the growth of plants. As a result the vegetables appear healthy but lose their nutritional value and taste. Similarly, medical practitioners prescribe supplements and vitamins to fertilize, boost human bodies. And business houses have been indiscriminately using *incentives* to fertilize actions! *Incentives* no doubt boost the actions of workers initially but later result in the decline of their work output. This problem has risen since the intellect is not sufficiently developed to conceive and promote the *initiative* in workers, essential for better production and real growth of the organisation.

Few realise that the free use of *incentives* increases gross selfishness among the workers. And the proliferation of personal desires, instead of a spirit of service to a common cause, proves cancerous to an organisation. It is a grave problem the modern business community faces. A problem that cannot be solved by abruptly discontinuing the use of *incentives* among the workforce. It has to be discreetly tackled by first introducing the concept of working for an ideal. In fact, the head of an organisation must lead the way himself by conceptualising the importance of an ideal, setting a proper one and working towards it. Thereafter, educate the workers to conceive and follow it in practice along with him. Thus the idea of a common cause must be gradually nourished and nurtured in an organisation by the leader. The members of that organisation would then develop the *initiative* to work for the cause. The emergence of *initiative* in due course displaces the dependence upon *incentives* to promote work. As a result the production in the unit would shoot up. The *initiative* can further be increased by the intellect pitching up higher and higher ideals. Business houses with such service oriented workforce would then diverge to greater dimension instead of their present trend of converging and fading out of existence.

Formula for Success

Productivity in business is directly related to success. In fact success is measured by increase in productivity.

There is a clamour for success all over the world. But few have attempted to define success and find out the true inputs to effectively achieve it.

The first lesson to learn about success is that it is an *effect*. And an *effect* belongs to the future. Everyone longs for success. Wishes to gain the *effect* without really going into its *cause*. Not realising that every *effect* has a *cause*. That you reap what you sow. It is an impeccable law. But the mass of humanity craves for the fruit without even planting the seed. You therefore need to attend to the cause for gaining success. And the cause for success is appropriate action. If your action is proper, perfect it would result in success. If improper, imperfect it would be a failure. In truth, your present action itself transforms into success or failure at a future period of time depending upon its quality.

An ideal action is made up of three essential constituents:

1. Concentration
2. Consistency
3. Cooperation.

A practitioner of these three disciplines has the appropriate action to command success in his field of operation. Productivity in business requires continual intellectual supervision while applying these rudiments of success. These three words may be used liberally in management lobbies but few have gone into their deeper import. Much less put them into practice. You therefore need to thoroughly understand these concepts. And apply them in your business.

Concentration

Concentration is the art of focusing the mind in the present. The human mind has a natural tendency to slip into worry of the past or anxiety for the future. Concentration is the technique exercised by your intellect to hold the mind on the present action without allowing it to slip into the past or future. You would need a powerful intellect to keep the mind focused. Concentration is measured by the extent the intellect engages the mind in the present.

Consistency

The second discipline is to be consistent in what you do. Having set an ideal to reach for, a goal to achieve your actions should flow in that direction. But there is a problem in maintaining this flow because the mind is prone to stray into other attractions. You need a strong intellect to overcome the mind's distractions and keep the actions going in the set direction. This technique of channelising your actions towards the goal is consistency. The practice of consistency lends power, strength to your action. You observe this clearly in nature. Water flowing in one direction has power. So does wind blowing in one direction. And light focused to a point. Thus through consistency your actions turn powerful.

A simple example taken from sports would illustrate the part played by consistency in achieving success. Consider an international tennis star being inconsistent in his practice of the game. Being often drawn to playing other games he fails to keep up with the rigorous practice that international competition demands. He would then be deprived of success in his field regardless of his proficiency in the game.

Cooperation

The third discipline is cooperation. To achieve an objective you need a spirit of cooperative endeavour. It is difficult to be successful and productive in a business without the active cooperation of colleagues. This principle applies to companies, communities and countries. Germany and Japan were devastated in the last World War. No sooner the war ended than the nationals pooled their efforts cooperatively to rebuild their nations. They returned to power and strength both economically and politically. The United States and Australia could boast of nothing a little over two hundred years back. The early settlers had to pool their resources in a spirit of cooperative endeavour to build their nations. Both have emerged as powerful nations of the world. Thus the third essential requirement for success is met with when the intellect maintains a true spirit of cooperation among those concerned in the business.

Maintaining the above three disciplines your actions should spell success and productivity in any field of endeavour.

CHAPTER IX

ESSENCE OF LEADERSHIP

The Leader

A leader should be well versed in the field of his activity. Possess a thorough knowledge of the subject of his business and an overall intelligence of all departments of his organisation. Which would be essential for him to effectively guide, direct his team. With his position and knowledge a true leader bears a humble countenance. Knowledge always goes with humility. Possessing such traits he would attract the adoration of his colleagues at office. And the members of that organisation naturally develop a team spirit for its success and progress.

Another essential quality of a leader is the ability to lead his team. He does not merely point out the way.

He actually goes forward, treads the path himself for others to follow. Oliver Goldsmith, an English poet, compares this trait to a bird teaching its offspring to fly. In his poem *The Village Preacher*, Goldsmith portrays a perfect human being in the life of a village preacher. In exquisite poetry he draws the comparison of the preacher's quality of leadership to that of a bird. When the mother bird knows its fledglings are ready to fly into the open skies it carefully draws them out of the nest. It tries each art of teaching, reproaches their delay in action, allures them to a brighter and beautiful life ahead and leads the way to it. So does the village preacher help his people by his own example to leave their selfish enclave and enjoy the brighter world of freedom and happiness. The quote:

> And, as a bird each fond endearment tries
> To tempt its new-fledged offspring to the skies,
> He tried each art, reproved each dull delay,
> Allured to brighter worlds and led the way.

A leader needs to follow this example. To lead and not just show the way to his colleagues at work. Parents especially must learn this trait and apply it while relating to their children. Set the standard of life for them to emulate. And not just give sermons. But in the modern world most parents commit a double fault. They do not live the life that they expect of their children and merely shower them with unsolicited advices. As a result the young remain repressed, frustrated or leave their homes.

A leader again is one whom you look up to, adore. He possesses adequate knowledge, fine emotion and a sense of service and sacrifice. With such adorable qualities he stands out like a beacon for others to emulate.

Above all, a leader fixes an ideal for himself and his team to work for. The ideal must be above self-centred motives to embrace the welfare of the larger community. To serve a higher cause in and through his business. The leader pursues the set ideal with a firm conviction. That attitude creates the initiative among the workforce to put forth the best for the organisation. Where there is no such ideal the members of the organisation have to be coerced to work through incentives. A practice which runs against business ethics.

Characteristics of Leadership

The fundamental characteristic of a leader is his ability to observe the sublime motto in action: *To strive, to struggle, not to succeed.* A leader's accent should rest on work and work alone. Just doing what he ought to do. Fulfilling his obligatory duty and responsibility. His intellect keeping the mind focused on the present action. Not allowing it to hang on to future results. Not becoming anxious, apprehensive, restless with the thought of success. He thus maintains the strain of work as worship with no concern of the fruit thereof. Such work turns out perfect, productive.

A leader has also to be aggressive not passive, dynamic not lackadaisical in his approach to work while he maintains mental equanimity and composure. But the problem with the modern leaders is that they are unable to combine both. Those that are active and progressive in their profession lack peace and contentment. While the peaceful and contented ones lack dynamism in action. This paradox runs through individuals, communities and nations. Action and peace seem to elude each other. That being so businesspersons and professionals who claim to be successful suffer from mental fatigue and stress. Hence their actions need to be carefully monitored by a powerful intellect. In not letting the mind's impulses and emotions disturb its concentration.

The intellect exercises its power to ensure the mind remains focused and the actions reach the set goal.

Oliver Goldsmith, in his poem *The Village Preacher* referred to earlier, describes this grand trait of objectivity in the preacher. A trait that every leader needs to possess for effective management. The preacher in the poem has chaste emotions which he liberally shares with his followers. He gives his heart away to them but never lets his feelings disturb the serenity of his head. He does not allow the emotions of his mind to interfere with thought, reason and judgement of his intellect. The poet draws a striking comparison of such a person to a tall cliff. A cliff rises well above the rolling clouds with its peak ever in contact with the sun. The clouds refer to emotions that gather in the breast, mind while the peak refers to the intellect which is ever attuned to wisdom, the sun above. This metaphor is acclaimed in literary lobbies as among the best in English literature. The quote:

> *To them his heart, his love, his griefs were given,*
> *But all his serious thoughts had rest in Heaven.*
> *As some tall cliff that lifts its awful form,*
> *Swells from the vale, and midway leaves the storm,*
> *Though round its breast the rolling clouds are spread,*
> *Eternal sunshine settles on its head.*

Besides the internal disturbances of the mind, an executive may face external calls and appeals which could distract him from pursuing the set course of action. In such situations he must exercise objectivity to deny his participation in other activities if he is convinced that his work will be impaired.

Another characteristic of a leader is the absence of a complex, either superiority or inferiority. A person develops a complex when he lays the accent on his ego rather than the composite whole of the organisation he works for. An arrogant claim of superiority is as absurd as a despondent feeling of inferiority. Either feeling causes mental agitation, suffering. Why have any complex? Everyone has a distinct role to play in this world. So have you. None is big or small. Important or unimportant. Learn to accept yourself as you are, a part of the whole. Live by it. You will then be free from the menace of complexes.

Ralph Waldo Emerson in his poem vide *The Mountain and the Squirrel* exposes the absurdity of individuals sporting complexes. Each possesses a talent of his own. Why compare one with another. Just play your part impersonally as best as you can. There is no need to entertain an air of superiority or inferiority.

Attitudes in Leadership

A few of the attitudes in leadership listed below are: Sense of Dispassion, Spirit of Service and Sacrifice, Identification, Empathy.

Sense of Dispassion

An essential attitude of a leader is to maintain a sense of dispassion right through his leadership. Where the head rules the heart. When the intellect holds its suzerainty over the impulses and ravings of the mind. A leader cannot afford to let his actions be driven directly by the passions of the mind without applying the discretion of the intellect.

A plant is bereft of emotion. An animal has emotions which drive its actions since it lacks an intellect. Whereas a human possesses emotions as well as an intellect to direct his action through reason and judgement. A perfect human being is one who has emotion but is not emotional. Has passion but is not passionate. Has sentiment but is not sentimental. A leader therefore should use the intellect to lead his team with dispassionate passion, with disinterested interest in the conduct of his business.

A sports captain places the success of the team above his individual performance. Where there is conflict of interest between that of the team and his personal contribution he sacrifices his individual stake for his team's success. So does the captain of a ship sacrifice his person for his passengers. A leader should thus demonstrate his objectivity for the wellbeing of his organisation.

Spirit of Service and Sacrifice

A leader's obligation lies in merely performing his duty and responsibility without polluting it with personal motives. Just doing what he ought to do. Without appending any prefixes or suffixes to action. His actions then command strength and power.

A leader must maintain a spirit of service and sacrifice in his workforce. Dedicate his work for the wellbeing of the organisation even at the expense of personal interest. Sacrifice the lower for the higher. Learn this lesson from the divine expression of nature. Everything in the cosmos works on the principle of service and sacrifice. The sun gives vitality. The clouds provide rain. Earth yields vegetation. Nightingale sings. Rose gives fragrance. With no axe to grind.

A leader must emulate this magnificence of nature. And learn to serve his organisation dispassionately for its overall growth. Take up the grand stand of nature. Give rather than take. Few realise the grandeur and power of serving, giving. The more you give the more you gain is the inexorable law of life reiterated by Swami Rama Tirtha: *The way to gain anything is to lose it.*

Identification, Empathy

A leader establishes his authority, power more through identification with, feelings for his colleagues rather than his position or status in the company. The natural feeling of empathy for fellow workers brings about a rapport, a spirit of cooperation. The emotion of love also creates an atmosphere of understanding among the workforce. Such feeling and understanding fosters the attitude of service and sacrifice.

The members of a unit develop empathy, a sense of oneness when they consider themselves as mere spokes in a wheel. That they are all together to constitute the unit. Such a beauteous attitude of togetherness running through a unit displaces the egoistic thought of either indispensability or dispensability in its members.

Qualities of a Leader

Of the three mental temperaments *sattvik*, *rajasik* and *tamasik* that constitute a human being, a leader needs to be predominantly *sattvik*, the foremost of them. It is a state of mind in equanimity, serenity, composure, objectivity. He must avoid the *rajasik* temperament when the mind becomes impulsive, passionate, agitated. Also keep clear off the *tamasik* temperament which is being lackadaisical, indifferent, procrastinating.

An inevitable quality of a leader is wielding a sharp intellect. A well-developed intellect provides the clarity of the overall operation of the company and his particular role in it. A clarity that enables him to make quick decisions, choose the right course of action and promptly execute it. Not let his mind prevaricate, procrastinate any issue pertaining to his business. Put off work for the future which can be done right now in the present. Thus using a powerful intellect a leader maintains his objectivity while running the business. Never letting the impulses and emotions of his mind disturb his vision and decision making.

Two more essential qualities that a leader needs to possess are concentration and consistency. Concentration is the art of the intellect holding the mind on present action without allowing it to slip into the past or future. Concentration is a basic ingredient for achieving success in any field of activity. It is all the more important for a leader to acquire and practise this trait. The second quality, consistency is the skill of channelising one's actions towards the goal set to achieve. Consistency is impaired when the mind is drawn toward other attractions while pursuing the goal. Here again a leader uses his intellect to control the mind from being distracted and direct actions along his line of pursuit.

Yet another important trait that a leader must possess is a sense of proportion. A sense of proportion is distinct and different from a sense of values. A leader's sense of values may be perfect. However, in practical life these values have to be applied appropriately, placed with the right perspective in his plan of action. A leader no doubt prioritises his pending tasks and executes the items of work accordingly. But on occasions when a person, situation or environment needs an immediate or special attention he uses the sense of proportion to accommodate the particular exigency. Having the right values is like having the right medicine for an illness. But the medicine will be of little use to the patient unless administered in the right dosage. So does the application of the sense of proportion become an essential aspect while following the sense of values.

Obligations of a Leader

A leader's first obligation is to conceptualise his objective and prepare a proper plan of action to achieve it. People all over have a general tendency to plan their work *forward* – day-to-day, week-to-week, month-to-month without a clear picture of the overall objective. Instead, the leader must estimate the time available for the project at hand and plan *backward* for its completion. If the project is to be completed in the stipulated time, fix the quantum of work that has to be covered in half that time. Next, in the first quarter. And what needs to be done this year, this month, this week, today. Thus must you plan and work *backward*. Split the time and work into multiple frames and clear each frame. You should then achieve your objective with ease.

Having set a clear plan of action a leader is obliged to lead the way for his colleagues to pursue. Using a sharp intellect he takes quick decisions and follows through forthwith with action. He is punctual and methodic in executing his plan of action. He thus sets a standard and a definite procedure for his teammates to emulate.

154

Again, a leader working in an organisation cannot afford to carry an egoistic feeling that he can handle everything himself. He must consider himself a part of the whole. And discreetly delegate whatever work can be delegated and follow up until it is completed. Delegation is not shirking work by passing the buck on to another. It means an intelligent distribution and coordination of work among those involved in it. It helps to bring about better relationship and output of work.

In the process of delegating work to colleagues a leader should locate individual talents among them for assuming greater responsibility in the organisation. And graft the necessary training procedure in their work culture. Thus must he ensure substitutes are prepared to take over higher responsibilities in all departments of work. A true leader therefore is one who never makes himself indispensable. That is rendered possible when his interest lies in the overall growth and welfare of his organisation.

Another obligation is for the leader to be accessible to his colleagues. It would serve the interest of the organisation to maintain a spirit of camaraderie among the workers. He needs to be familiar but not too close, vulgar. He should maintain the dignity of a CEO even as he is approachable. Free accessibility at all levels of management would create the right employer-employee relationship. And effective communication among the ranks for their better performance.

That brings up another obligation of a leader. A supervisor is responsible to communicate properly leaving no ambiguity. The problem in communication is not really envisaged by supervisors constantly engaged in instructing others. And the need to ensure proper communication is much less appreciated. Where there is a failure in following instructions the supervisor must accept that he has faulted. It is the primary duty and responsibility of the instructor to ensure the one receiving his instruction has got it beyond a shadow of doubt. A leader should realise the importance of communication. It needs precaution and precision in exercising it. A simple error in execution can lead a business to adverse consequences.

The difficulty in conveying instructions to others can be practically demonstrated in a workshop. The demonstration would need four persons from the delegates. It is about passing a message, one to another and each giving it out to the delegates assembled in the workshop. A telephonic message from a husband at work to his wife at home, as follows:

"Darling, I am speaking to you from my office. Both of us have been invited for an official party which is at the Hyatt Regency at seven this evening. Sorry I forgot to mention to you yesterday. I would not have the time to come home and get back. I suggest you take a cab and reach the hotel directly. After the party we could go home together in my car. I will meet you at the lounge at quarter to seven. I am wearing a navy suit and a maroon tie if you wish to wear something to match!"

Distribute this message in print to each of the delegates keeping the four persons out. Call one of the four and give him this message orally before the delegates assembled there so that they also hear its contents. After receiving the message he goes out and passes it on again orally to the second person. The second one now comes back to the audience and delivers what he has heard. This exercise of listening and delivering the message is repeated from the second to the third and from the third to the fourth person. The fourth, having received the very same message, now comes before the audience to deliver the original message that the husband gave to his wife. You will be amused to hear the hilarious distortions of the original. And how the substance of the message invariably gets mutilated in the process of communication. Such is the difficulty in communicating a simple message. Business executives should therefore bear this in mind and exercise caution while instructing their colleagues at work.

Above all obligations, a leader is responsible to maintain the right mental atmosphere in his organisation. A spirit of cooperative endeavour. What the layperson understands as team spirit. He achieves this through a blend of proper understanding of his colleagues and the necessary emotion to go with it.

CHAPTER X

SETTING RELATIONSHIPS RIGHT

In life, be it business or family, you need to relate properly to whomever and whatever you contact. A lack of proper relationship would lead you to frustration and build up your stress. Ironically, people take utmost care to choose the 'right partner', official or domestic, but quite ignore the importance of the 'right relation' with that person. It is not *whom* or *what* you meet in life that matters but *how* you meet it. The great Greek philosopher, Socrates drives home this point brilliantly. A young man sought the master's opinion about his decision to get married. The master shot out his advice, "By all means get married, if you do get a good wife you will be happy, if you get a bad one you will become a philosopher!" So all through life your accent is on finding the right partner or environment instead of learning the art of relating to it.

A knife is indispensable in a home. The family uses it everyday in the kitchen. But the same knife has been put to a horrifying use of stabbing a member of the family. A knife per se cannot be labelled as beneficial or detrimental to the user. It would depend upon how one relates to it. So is it with any partnership. If you relate to the person wisely you create a heaven out of the relationship. If not, your unintelligent relationship turns hellish. Heaven and hell are therefore not geographical places. They are mere states of your mind. You make yourself. You mar yourself. You are the architect of your fortune. You are the architect of your misfortune. All you need to do is set a right, healthy relationship with the world you contact.

Streamline Your Relation

In the course of life you meet different types of people, situations and environments. When your intellect is weak your mind is affected by external fluctuations. You become upset. But with a strong intellect you could deal with them objectively. Understand their inherent nature and relate to them appropriately.

Whenever you cannot change the flow, get into the flow and make the best out of it. A bad workman complains of his tools. Be a perfect craftsman, get on to your job with the tools you have. Be a master, not a slave to external challenges. You then maintain your objectivity in life. As you lose objectivity, the intellect's control over the mind, you become impulsive. And with further loss of control of the mind you could turn eccentric, even hysterical. End up in a pathetic equation with the world.

As the intellect loses its strength the mind takes over your personality. Your mind becomes emotionally involved, obsessed with the business at work and attached, infatuated with the family at home. This sickening state of mind is the killer of all relationships. It ruins your success and progress at work, your peace and happiness at home. When the mind is overwhelmed with impulses and emotions the intellect becomes ineffectual. As a result business is impaired. At home, spouses become infatuated to one another. And suffer from severe attachment and possessiveness. They get suffocatingly close and their relationship ends up in separation. Kahlil Gibran, the Lebanese American philosopher puts this idea across beautifully: *Marriage is like a temple resting on two pillars. If they come too close to each other the temple will collapse.* Your affection therefore should not be restricted to the members of your family alone. Your home should be the centre and not the boundary of your affection.

To set your relationships right with the world at large you need to observe certain disciplines. They are fundamental human controls and restraints which help build sound and healthy relationship. When these are neglected any relationship would wither and come to an end. A few of the disciplines are covered herein.

Selfless and Selfish

The character of a person is determined by the measure of selflessness in him. The more unselfish he is the finer, the nobler his character. Such a person would maintain a proper and peaceful relation with his contacts. That explains why all unselfish persons are contented and happy. And the selfish mentally agitated and unhappy. Humans all over suffer from stress because of their self-centredness. When A meets B, he entertains the thought, 'what can I get out of B'. The same thought runs through B, 'what can I get out of A'. The virus of selfishness destroys the relationship in persons.

The influx of selfishness in humans has gradually eroded the thought of duty and responsibility among them. The trend everywhere is to insist on rights rather than fulfilling one's obligations in life. Unethical legal claims is the order of the day. Marital relationships have collapsed because of this selfish attitude towards each other. Either spouse has lost the concept of duty to the other. Instead, each finds possible ways and means to establish his or her right. An attitude which has taken its toll on marital harmony around the world. It is a natural law that relationships built on rights shall perish. And those built on duties flourish.

Another trait of selfishness prevalent in the society is to 'take' from others, to 'grab' whatever comes in one's way. For an organisation, a society to survive each of its members must want to give, serve, help the unit rather than helping oneself. Right from the leader downwards the trend of thought should be to serve, to sacrifice. Not merely to exploit others and amass wealth. This mental climate created by the thought of sharing would bring about prosperity and progress in the community. In simple words, practise the art of saying 'après vous, after you' in every transaction of your life.

While relating to children, parents exhibit their selfishness again in the form of attachment and possessiveness. They mentally bind themselves to their children and suffocate them with possessiveness. A trait dominated by the mind while the intellect plays no part. Their possessiveness crushes the young with undue supervision and uncalled-for sermons. Parents the world over suffer from this deadly trait. They virtually ride on the backs of their kids. No kid can take this constant humiliation. The natural outcome of such domination is confrontation or separation. No wonder the young leave their homes soon after they reach their maturity.

Proper Assessment

The beauty and grandeur of humans is in wielding a powerful intellect all through their life. Then their relationship with the world would be perfect. But the grave problem that humanity faces is the lack of development and use of the intellect. As a result their attachment and possessiveness has reached the level of animals. Human beings have lost their objectivity, the decorum and dignity of their race. The rehabilitation of the intellect would need time. However, your present intellect could be used to improve your relationships through proper assessment of the contacts you make.

Primarily, you must assess the nature of those who are in close contact with you. Your spouse, your children, colleagues, friends. With proper assessment of each one's character you would know the type of behaviour to expect from the person concerned. And thus maintain a right relationship with one and all. Without such assessment your expectations would become unreasonable and your relationship turn foul.

Control and Regulation

Sexual relationship also serves as a binding factor between partners living together. But both lack the objectivity to use it wisely to strengthen their relationship. Their minds crave for the instant pleasure it provides. When the intellect is undeveloped it lacks the power to regulate their sexual demand. As a result they indiscriminately yield and indulge in it. And soon lose the pleasure thereof and its binding influence in their relationship.

To streamline all sensual contacts the intellect must exercise control over the demands of the senses. Avoid the mind's excessive indulgence in them. None seem to realise that indulgence in sense objects diminishes the pleasures derived therefrom. And those who indulge indiscriminately become neutralised. They lose the pleasure completely. Their relationship then becomes mechanical, even repulsive. The wise should avoid this predicament by regulating and moderating their sensual activities. That would ensure freshness in their relationship with the world right through life.

Art of Parenting

Parents have a difficult time relating to their children. They bitterly complain about 'their independent and impertinent behaviour'. That they have gone out of control and stopped relating to them. Almost all parents point their finger at the young and see no fault of their own. Little do they realise that the problem of relationship invariably emanates from parents. From their clinging attachment and possessiveness towards the children. In the absence of the intellect the constant emotional pressures exerted by them virtually strangulate the young. The first step to straighten relations is for the parents to realise their inherent weakness and make a careful study of the psychological traits of their children.

Children are born with the capacity to absorb knowledge from the external world. It is called *udana* in Sanskrit language. *Udana*, the power of grasping fresh knowledge is maximum at birth and it diminishes with age. And when a person reaches ripe old age it practically disappears. That explains why youngsters absorb ideas and ideologies, trends and fashions faster while the older folks take much longer time. The disparity in time for such absorption causes what people term as a generation gap. With the result the old perceive the world differently from the young.

This disparity leads to argument and altercation, confrontation and conflict between parents and their children. Neither of them is aware of this natural discrepancy. If either one understands that the other helplessly manifests his own nature then one would be tolerant and adjust one's relation amicably. If both understand this simple phenomenon of nature and conduct themselves accordingly they would live in perfect harmony. But the problem humans face everywhere is the lack of such understanding on both sides which has strained, practically destroyed parent-child relationship.

Moreover, children possess extraordinary energy. Effervesce with tireless passion and play. The older ones, parents lack energy and enthusiasm in life. They are prone to become tired, fatigued. And try to combat it with stimulants, weekend breaks and vacations. The reason for this contrast is the absence of worry and anxiety in children. While adults are plagued with worries of the past and anxieties for the future.

Parents are not aware of this stark reality. In their desperation to exercise control over the children's tireless activities they suffocate them with incessant restrictions and restraints. The solution to the problem lies not in stifling them thus. But in studying their natural tendencies and giving their energy a direction. This is possible when the adults possess knowledge of the higher values of life and practise them. By themselves living those values and educating the children, the parents should help the children's energies flow in the right direction instead of stifling them.

This procedure in dealing with family confrontations is akin to controlling road accidents. Where too many accidents take place there are two ways of avoiding them. One way, which is no way, is to reduce the speed limit of vehicles to a ridiculously low level. The other, sensible way is to provide drivers with proper road sense by educating them with traffic rules and regulations. So too, youngsters should be provided with value education rather than being showered with do's and don'ts. The general trend in the world is that parents fail to set examples of right living but merely pester their children with ill-founded advices. To set the relationship right they will have to live the life they wish their young to follow and avoid giving them sermons. The late president of the United States, Abraham Lincoln had put this idea across succinctly: *There is just one way to bring up a child in the way he should go and that is to travel that way yourself.*

Therefore it is incumbent upon parents to set the standards through right examples for their children to follow. A few examples set herein should serve as general guidelines.

Freedom and Licence

Growth in a field of activity is enhanced in an atmosphere of freedom. Children would need that freedom for their growth and progress in life. However, freedom should not be misconstrued as licence. Parents must clearly understand the difference between freedom and licence. When freedom crosses its limits, breaks norms and standards, rules and regulations it becomes licentiousness. Children need to be educated on this difference and given the freedom to operate. But when parents tread on their legitimate freedom the relationship turns sour.

Fight Ego

Ego is a dreadful trait in a human being. It is one's arrogation of 'I' and 'me'. The common demonstration of this trait is a glaring assertion of one's views, more often unsolicited. 'I don't agree', 'I don't like it', 'I beg to differ' and the like. Also personalising everything, a constant reference to 'me'. 'What about me'.

Another characteristic of the ego is one's sense of possessiveness. A demeaning quality inconsistent with the dignity of a human being. The constant declaration of 'my' and 'mine', even when not threatened by others' claims, mars the charisma of a person. It interferes, even spoils the harmonious relationship among people. It is a trait that breaks the bond of affection and camaraderie. Adults do not realise the negative effects of their possessive nature and freely indulge in the use of 'my' and 'mine'. To make matters worse parents encourage children to fix signboards on their room doors with their names or 'My room' on them. Sometimes with a suffix 'Don't enter'. These perpetrations, most times innocent, build an ego from childhood which disturbs the peace and harmony in relationships.

Fix Ideal

Humans stand out from all other creatures in their ability to rise above the ego and egocentric desires. To serve and sacrifice for others. To attune to this great quality one has to fix an ideal to work for. An ideal is something beyond one's self-centred interest in life, above one's selfishness to merely fulfil personal desires. It is directed to the welfare of the community, the wellbeing of one and all. Children need to be trained from the very beginning to think on these lines. To work for a common cause, for a benevolent purpose above one's selfish interest. As the young learn and practise working for a higher ideal in life, their character and behavioural pattern shapes beautifully. The society in which they work develops a spirit of giving rather than taking. And an atmosphere of service and sacrifice prevails therein.

Surrender and Gratitude

Surrender, followed by gratitude, is an essential quality that every human needs to possess. The onus lies on the elders to educate their young on this trait. One must understand the importance of surrendering to areas of one's ignorance. If you do not possess the knowledge of medicine you must surrender to one equipped with that knowledge. Seek the help of a doctor. If you do not know engineering you must take the help of an engineer. If however you do not care to surrender to those knowledgeable in the realm of your ignorance you could meet with adverse consequences. Surrender does not mean blind acceptance. Whatever advice you seek, examine it carefully with your intellect and accept that which admits reason and judgement.

Another gross behaviour prevalent in modern society proceeds from the lack of gratitude. Gratitude is one's silent, genuine acknowledgement of any form of service, benefit received. A life without it deprives humans of one of their noblest traits. Gratitude is something that could rate even higher than love and kindness. Much like clearing a debt would rank above an act of charity. But it is rather unfortunate that this magnificent trait is virtually obsolete in the present world. One takes the help of another, it could be surgery in an emergency, and sues the surgeon for the slightest, unintended error. William Shakespeare in his play *Julius Caesar* unequivocally denounces ingratitude as stronger than traitors' arms. Where ingratitude infiltrates a society, the society

172

putrefies. There would be stress and strain, disharmony and disturbance among its members. Children cannot afford to grow up in such an atmosphere. The adults must realise this and set the right ambience through surrender and gratitude.

CHAPTER XI

THE ULTIMATE MANAGEMENT

Management encompasses every part, facet and phase of human life. It is not restricted to business and family as understood by people in general. One could be operating one's business successfully, maintaining harmony with the family and yet go wrong in managing several other aspects of life. Leaving one with a host of lingering desire and expectation, worry and anxiety, stress and strain in everyday life. But a human, being the supreme most of species, has the competence to gain complete suzerainty over the world. A status that could be achieved by self-management. A mastery over one's own self.

Hierarchy in Management

In the execution of line management the higher

level of authority exercises control over the lower. It would therefore be necessary to study the echelons of management in human affairs. The levels start from the physical body and rise gradually to the supreme Self within.

The body is controlled, governed by the mind. Where and when the mind does not apply itself, the body and its organs of perception and action cease to function. As is evident in deep-sleep. But the mind has no control over its direction or dimension. It can drive perception and action to any limits. Make life grossly materialistic and sensual. It could break ethical and legitimate barriers to amass wealth and power and develop possessiveness. The mind per se has no means of regulating or moderating its movement even at the point of extinction.

The vagaries of the mind can however be controlled by the intellect. The intellect occupies a higher level of authority than the mind. A well-developed intellect can give the mind the right direction and a realistic goal to pursue and attain. But the situation in the world today presents a mass of people following a herd instinct without such an intellect to guide the mind. Humanity needs to attend to this pressing situation. Failing which there would be further altercation and anarchy in the world. The intellect must therefore be developed and used to bring about sound management in all aspects of life.

Furthermore, human beings are privileged with the possession of the subtle-intellect known in Sanskrit language as *sukshma buddhi*. Whose range goes beyond the terrestrial realm to reach the transcendental Reality. Whereas the intellect that is used to manage the affairs of the world is known as *tikshna buddhi*, gross-intellect. The subtle-intellect is the next higher level in the hierarchy of management. A human alone is empowered to use it to contact the transcendental Reality which is omnipresent, omniscient, omnipotent. Which the populace has from time immemorial designated as God. The all-pervading God can however be located in the Self within. It is similar to locating the government of a country at its capital. The government no doubt pervades all over the country but one needs to go to the capital to contact it.

The supreme Reality is inconceivable even by humans. But the subtle-intellect posits the Reality as something that transcends the terrestrial world. And helps you further to contact It in the Self within. In terms of management a fully developed gross-intellect could at best deal with and exercise control over mundane matters. Thus achieve for you all management within the realm of this world. Whereas the subtle-intellect helps you identify with the supreme Self within. When the identification with the Self is complete, you become one with the Self. Gain total suzerainty over the world. Attain the ultimate management.

The subtle-intellect empowers a human to identify with the Self. The Self is the Living-Principle, Conscious-Principle, pure Consciousness which enlivens the matter vestures to manifest as living beings. It is homogeneous, the unifying principle in the heterogeneous creatures of the world. It acts like electricity, the one energy manifesting differently in the manifold electric gadgets. In effect, living creatures can be classified under three main species – plant, animal and human. A plant possesses the Self and body with no mind, no gross-intellect or subtle-intellect. Whereas an animal possesses the Self, body, mind and a rudimentary gross-intellect but no trace of the subtle-intellect. A human being alone has the Self pulsating through all the four equipments. The presence of the subtle-intellect renders a human the chef d'oeuvre of creation. The subtle-intellect helps identify with the Self to gain complete mastery over the universe. The different constitutions of the three species are demarcated graphically as follows:

	Body	Mind	Gross Intellect	Subtle Intellect	Self
Plant	✓	✗	✗	✗	✓
Animal	✓	✓	✗	✗	✓
Human	✓	✓	✓	✓	✓

The plant, possessing merely a body, is totally dependent upon the external world. But the animal with its mind and a rudimentary gross-intellect could to an extent manage the rigours of nature. However, it is largely dependent upon the environment and situation around and about it. Distinct from other creatures, the human species is privileged with both gross and subtle-intellects to meet the challenges of the world, even rise above and conquer it.

Identifying and operating with the gross-intellect you could use its power to manage, overcome the challenges that the world confronts you with. But then you remain very much with the sea of challenges, time and again clearing them only to gain temporary peace and satisfaction. Rare indeed is the wise one who identifies with the subtle-intellect to reach the supreme Self, the ultimate in the echelon of management. Realising the Self and revelling in absolute peace and fulfilment you become the monarch of all you survey.

Human beings are born in the world and borne by nature only to gain *Identity* with Self, to attain the *Supremacy* of Self and reach the *Ultimatum* of Self.

Gain Identity with Self

To identify with someone or something you need to send your thoughts in that direction. And when your thoughts are firmly established in it you become one with it. The law of nature is such: *As you think so you become.* When your thoughts constantly run towards your body you become a physical person. Thereafter you operate from the physical level. With hardly any emotional, intellectual or spiritual expression. You merely run after material wealth and sensual pleasures. You live at the grossest level of the human personality.

In the next level you could identify with the mind and its emotions, feelings. The more you identify with the mind and less with the intellect you would become impulsive, eccentric, even turn hysterical, insane. But by identifying with and using your gross-intellect you render yourself free from these emotional tantrums. And when the gross-intellect is strong and powerful you would ride over the obstacles and challenges of the world. Your life would then be organised to balance action and peace.

Above all, the rare one uses the subtle-intellect to identify with the Self. Realises the Self. The pinnacle of all management, all control. The world then ceases to be an adversary. The Self-realised, Enlightened Soul operating from the Self establishes complete suzerainty over the universe.

Attain Supremacy of Self

In order of superiority, the physical body is the grossest of the human equipments. The mind is subtler, superior to the body. The mind controls the body and its actions. Higher than the mind is the gross-intellect which can control the mind and its emotions, body and its actions. All these controls however pertain to the affairs of the world. But a human being possesses the superior most of all equipments, the subtle-intellect. You could use the subtle-intellect to rise above the world by drawing the divinity within you. By asserting the supreme Self within and negating the matter vestures. By maintaining a constant awareness of Self:

I am the Self, not this body.

I am the Self, not this mind.

I am the Self, not this gross-intellect.

I am the Self, not this subtle-intellect.

Thus must you identify with the Self while you perceive and act with your body, feel emotions with your mind, comprehend thoughts with your intellect. You would gradually get attached to the Self and detached, liberated from constraints and limitations of the body, mind and intellect and their worldly entanglement. Reign supreme. Attain the supremacy of Self.

Reach Ultimatum of Self

The Self is the ultimate State of Being. The Experience transcending all that the terrestrial world can offer. The State of absolute satisfaction, contentment, satiation. While all terrestrial experiences are found wanting, limited, insatiable.

In the passage of life you fail to realise the absolute supremacy of your Self. Living in ignorance of Self you identify with the material layers of your personality. As a result you go through the perennial cycle of the waking, dream and deep-sleep states of consciousness. In the waking state you assume the character of the waker experiencing the waking world. In the dream state you assume the character of the dreamer experiencing the dream world. In the deep-sleep you become the deep-sleeper experiencing a void, nothing. The Self supports, pervades these three states and exists per se beyond them. The supreme State of the unmanifest Self above the three manifested states is known in Sanskrit as *turiya*. *Turiya* literally means 'fourth'. It is the fourth State of pure, unconditioned Consciousness that transcends the conditioned states of the waking, dream and deep-sleep. You belong to the unconditioned fourth State and not these conditioned states. You are the Self, not the waker, dreamer, deep-sleeper. When you are established therein you reach the Ultimate of human existence free from all conditioning. Become the omnipotent, omniscient, omnipresent

Self. Thereafter, you operate from Self. The entire world is at your beck and call.

To reach that transcendental State of Existence and attain the ultimate suzerainty over the world you may study the author's book *The Eternities: Vedanta Treatise.*

INDEX

Other Publications of
A. Parthasarathy

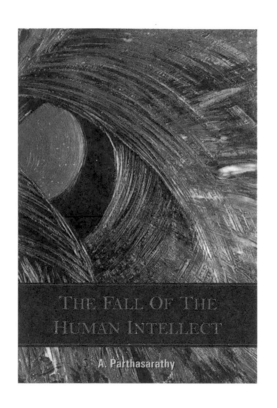

THE FALL OF THE
HUMAN INTELLECT

A. Parthasarathy

The Fall of the Human Intellect

135 Pages

Stress, depression, disease in individuals and militancy, vandalism, terrorism in societies is threatening humanity with extinction. The book traces back the source of this impending disaster to the continual neglect of the human intellect. It highlights the fundamental difference between intelligence and intellect. Intelligence is acquired from schools and universities while the intellect is developed through one's personal effort in thinking, reasoning, questioning before accepting anything. The book is designed to develop the intellect and save humanity from self-destruction.

The Eternities: Vedanta Treatise

351 Pages

The book expounds the ancient philosophy of Vedanta. It presents the eternal principles of life and living. Living is a technique that needs to be learnt and practised by one and all. The technique provides the formula for remaining active all through life while maintaining inner peace. It helps one develop a powerful intellect to meet the challenges of the world.

Above all, the Treatise helps one evolve spiritually. It provides the knowledge and guidance to reach the ultimate in human perfection. The goal of Self-realisation.

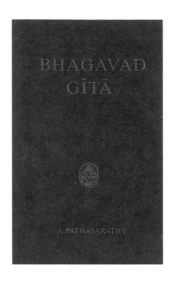

Bhagavad Gita

880 Pages

The Gita brings to light the positive and negative tendencies that lie within you. They are your higher aspirations and lower desires in life that effect your evolution or devolution. Its chaste philosophy helps you conquer desire and regain the supreme Self. The state of Godhood. The book comprises the text, transliteration, word-meaning, translation and commentary. A useful contribution is the topic-wise division of each chapter which helps you capture the thought-flow and message therein.

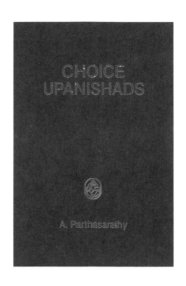

Choice Upanishads

243 Pages

The Upanishads form the final portion of the Vedas which are considered the primeval source of the scriptures. Sage Bādarāyaṇa Vyāsa classified them as Rik, Sāma, Yajuh and Atharvana Vedas. This book provides an exhaustive commentary on four Upanishads namely Kena, Īśāvāsya, Kaivalya and Muṇḍaka. The Upanishads expound a system of philosophy which helps humanity attain spiritual enlightenment.

Bhaja Govindam

75 Pages

A text by philosopher-saint Ādi Śaṅkarācārya that provides the basic instructions on life. It highlights the two main motivations which propel the life of a human being viz. acquisition and enjoyment. The first motivation drives him to acquire, aggrandise, hoard wealth. And the second causes him to indulge in the enjoyment of the acquired wealth. The text points out the hollowness of these external pursuits. Directs you to seek the supreme Self within. And reach the eternal Abode of peace and bliss.

Atmabodha

138 Pages

The text composed by Ādi Śaṅkarācārya presents a
gallery of several word paintings. Each depicts
a philosophical idea to help the seeker comprehend
the subtle theme of the scriptures. The commentary
elucidates its striking similes and metaphors taken
from nature and life. Together they prepare a
spiritual practitioner to gain the awareness of the
supreme Reality in all walks of life. And lead him to
the realisation of the supreme Self.

Select English Poems

123 Pages

A collection of twenty poems and excerpts from English literature. Includes selections from the works of William Shakespeare, Samuel Johnson, Oliver Goldsmith, John Milton, William Wordsworth and Matthew Arnold.

The book analyses each literary piece to derive the powerful messages encapsulated in it. It conveys the philosophical insights essential for maintaining peace and progress in life.

The Symbolism of Hindu Gods and Rituals

158 Pages

A practical text explaining the allegorical significance of gods and goddesses; rituals and festivals; invocations and prayers. It educates a spiritual aspirant on the philosophical aspect of religious practices.